DEMAND AND SUPPLY

DEMAND AND SUPPLY

BY

RALPH TURVEY

Economic Adviser, Scientific Control Systems Ltd

*Lately Joint Deputy Chairman, National Board for
Prices and Incomes, and sometime Chief Economist
The Electricity Council*

London
GEORGE ALLEN & UNWIN LTD
RUSKIN HOUSE   MUSEUM STREET

First published in 1971

ISBN   0 04 330198 3 *cased*
        0 04 330199 1 *paper*

Printed in Great Britain
in 11 point Baskerville type
by Alden & Mowbray Ltd
at the Alden Press, Oxford

To the staff of the
National Board for Prices and Incomes

Preface

This book is an introduction to the economics of resource allocation, often known as micro-economics. It is aimed both at the general reader and at A-level and first year university students. For such students it supplements the standard textbooks but does not replace them.

One feature of this book is that all the economics in it is applied economics. Theories which cannot be applied to British economic problems or which cannot be illustrated by British experience have been left out. It thus concentrates entirely on useful economics. This, incidentally, means that there are some seemingly odd omissions. I have been surprised to discover an apparent lack of convincing up-to-date and British evidence or illustration of some fairly familiar propositions. Rather than resort to quaint or foreign examples I have left these propositions out. But it is worth pointing out that a great deal of what economists think they know rests only on deduction rather than on hard fact.

The second particular feature of this book is that it only deals with the ways in which firms and households *do* behave. It is not about how they *should* behave, nor is it about how they *would* behave if various dubious hypotheses are made. In other words, there is no discussion of policy problems and no armchair theorizing.

Much of the information in the book comes from the

published reports of the late-lamented National Board for Prices and Incomes. Since this information was gathered mainly by the staff of that Board, I dedicate this book to them as a tribute to the quality of their work.

R.T.

Contents

CONTENTS

Chapter 1

CONSUMER DEMAND

Laymen sometimes use the word 'demand' to mean purchases or orders. In either case they are thinking of a single figure of, say, packets per month or tons per year. The economist, on the other hand, uses 'demand' in a special sense to indicate the whole set of factors determining purchases or orders. For him, demand is thus a relationship between the things that determine purchases on the one hand, and the amount people buy (or order) on the other. What interests him is the nature of this relationship; he asks what changes in what determinants will have which effects.

1.1. *The demand for margarine*

As an example, consider the demand for margarine. We could examine the demand for just one particular brand, such as Stork, but let us consider margarine in general. Fairly obviously, its demand is related to the demand for butter. Indeed if we look at Diagram 1 it is evident that consumer purchases of margarine plus butter taken together have been much more stable than consumer purchases of either taken separately. So one way of examining the demand for margarine is to look at it in two stages:

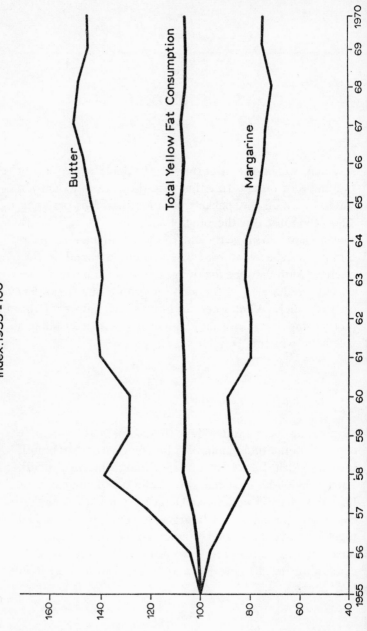

CONSUMPTION OF YELLOW FATS
Index: 1955 = 100

Butter

Total Yellow Fat Consumption

Margarine

– Demand for margarine plus butter;
– Share of margarine in this total.

The first stage involves looking at the demand for yellow fats. Eating habits are clearly an important factor here; presumably one reason why Americans buy less yellow fats per head per year than we do in Britain is that Americans do not eat bread and butter as much as we do.

The second stage involves more economics, so let us look at it in more detail. We do this by considering a number of factors which determine the share of margarine in total United Kingdom yellow fat purchases one by one. This involves supposing all relevant factors except one to remain unchanged, assuming the one we are concentrating on to alter, and enquiring how this will affect purchases. Thus we may ask: 'Other things equal, how will a change in the amount spent on advertising margarine affect total margarine purchases?'

This sort of question makes people tease economists for always assuming that other things remain equal when in fact they rarely do remain equal. But the assumption is just a scientific method of sorting out ideas, not a description of the world we live in. So we too shall take one thing at a time.

Our first 'thing' determining the demand for margarine versus butter is consumer preferences. This is a shorthand expression for the mixture of circumstances, habits, attitudes, likes and dislikes, knowledge and ignorance which dispose consumers towards the one or the other. Manufacturers spend a great deal of money trying to find out about consumer preferences so that they can tailor their products more closely to what people want. Since what they learn would help their competitors, they keep it secret and we can only guess at some of the facts they may have discovered.

A modern businessman would probably put down 'marketing' as the second factor determining the share of margarine. By this is meant the formulation of the product, its packaging, incentives to retailers to display it, advertising and so on. The practical business point is that these are all planned and decided together as part of a coherent policy to promote purchases of the brand. When a new brand is introduced, a big advertising campaign is required to launch it and retailers have to be persuaded to stock it. But all the same we can list some of these elements separately in our one-thing-at-a-time approach and put down the characteristics of the product – including its packaging – as our second set of factors determining the division of the yellow fat market between butter and margarine.

In this particular case the characteristics of the product have not been stationary. New brands have been introduced with new characteristics. Some time ago, margarine was just a cheap alternative to butter. But some of the new brands that have been launched over recent years appeal by virtue of their differences from butter, such as spreadability and convenient packs that can go straight on the table. These developments reflect research, both (as mentioned above) into consumer wants and into new ways of producing margarine. Some of the new brands even overlap butter in price. It is possible that it is these changes which explain the recent rise in the market share of margarine shown in Diagram 1.

Such changes through time in the quality of goods are easy to forget when we look only at total amounts as in the diagram. But a great deal of competitive effort in modern business is devoted to studying and trying to meet the preferences of consumers, and the economist who ignores it is neglecting a very important feature of the markets for consumer goods.

Our next factor is advertising. Other things equal, increased expenditure in advertising margarine – or decreased expenditure on advertising butter – will increase purchases of margarine at the expense of butter. It is perhaps a little less obvious that advertising affects sales not only via its effect on consumers but also via its effect on retailers. Their willingness to give space to Brand X may be increased if widespread advertising of it makes them feel that more customers are going to try it.

The main point to be made about the effect of advertising upon sales is that it is an effect which is extraordinarily difficult to predict. Indeed anyone who could make accurate predictions would rapidly make a fortune! To see how difficult it is, just consider all the links between the expenditure on a TV advertisement and its effect in stimulating purchases. The size of the TV audience at the time it is shown can be predicted fairly well and is in fact reflected in the cost of showing the advertisement. But how many of the audience will actually take in the message, how many of these will remember it and how many of these will actually buy who would not have bought if they had not seen the advertisement? Advertising agencies do serious research on these matters, but hunch still plays a major role. After all, there is no way of measuring the quality of an advertisement in advance of showing it.

Both margarine and butter are very widely available. So it is just for the sake of completeness that we add that the number of retail outlets counts too. If margarine were on sale at only half as many shops as butter was, margarine purchases would drop.

Next comes income. Its importance can be shown by figures from the 1969 Family Expenditure Survey showing the average weekly expenditures on butter and margarine by families of two adults and one child for families with different income levels. Expenditure is measured in shillings.

1969 EXPENDITURE OF 3-PERSON HOUSEHOLDS ON YELLOW FATS, BY INCOME GROUP					
Household weekly Income	£10 and under £20	£20 and under £25	£25 and under £30	£30 and under £40	£40 or more
Weekly expenditure on butter	3.1	3.0	3.6	3.4	3.9
Weekly expenditure on margarine	1.1	0.9	0.8	0.9	0.6

The pattern is not perfect, but it seems clear that the rich either buy more butter or buy higher quality butter (or both) than do the poor. As regards margarine, the tendency is the opposite. Since it seems unlikely that those who are well-off buy cheaper brands than those who are not, the tendency for expenditure on margarine to be lower when income is higher must mean that the quantity purchased is lower.

Margarine is not the only food which is bought in smaller quantities by those who are better off than by those who are poorer. Potatoes constitute another example and bread another. As living standards rise, people are able to afford a more varied diet and therefore concentrate less on such staples. In other words it is true both (i) that at any one time the rich, on average, eat less bread than the poor and (ii) that as people in general get richer as time passes they eat less bread. Between 1955 and 1968 total bread consumption fell by one-quarter in the UK. Goods such as bread are technically termed 'inferior' goods by economists.

The final factor affecting margarine purchases, and the one which most excites textbook writers, is price. Since margarine and butter are substitutes it is only common sense to say that, 'other things being equal', purchases of margarine will be stimulated either by a fall in margarine prices or by a rise in butter prices.

It would be nice if we could demonstrate the importance of prices by showing that margarine purchases have fallen and butter purchases have risen when the *ratio* of margarine prices to butter prices has risen. Unfortunately, this cannot be done – at least not in any simple way – for two reasons:

– 'Other things' were not equal;
– Butter and margarine prices in this country have not altered much in recent years.

Thus the probable price effects have been fairly mild, and have sometimes been offset and sometimes strengthened by advertising, by the introduction of new brands and by the gradual rise in real incomes. From 1968 to 1969 the average price paid for margarine by the eight thousand-odd families covered by the National Food Survey rose by one penny, while the average price paid for butter was almost unchanged. Yet the margarine share in total yellow fat purchases rose slightly.

Nevertheless the relative price effect must be important. The fact that Britain is the country in Western Europe with almost the highest ratio of butter consumption to margarine consumption cannot be unconnected with the fact that it has the *lowest* ratio of butter price to margarine price.

1.2. *The demand curve and its elasticity*

Economists are so convinced of the importance of prices as one of the factors determining purchases that they often divide these factors into just two groups:

– Price;
– Everything else.

They then assume 'everything else' to remain constant and think of demand as the relationship between the price and the amount bought. This is the famous demand curve. A change in purchases consequent upon a change in price is then a *movement along* this curve and a change consequent upon anything else is a *shift* of the whole curve.

Economists who are more mathematical prefer algebra to simple geometry and represent demand as a function relating purchases to several other things as well as price. This is what we have done, without using algebra, in discussing the demand for margarine. As a measure of the sensitivity of purchases to changes in the determining factors, economists use the concept of elasticity. Thus the strength of the effect of the price of a good upon the purchases of it is called the 'own-price elasticity of demand' (though the word 'own' is often omitted). It is defined as a ratio:

Proportional change in quantity
Proportional change in price

Thus if, other things remaining unchanged, a 10% rise in the average retail price of margarine leads to a 2% reduction in margarine sales, the own-price elasticity of demand for margarine is −0.2. If it leads to a 20% reduction, the elasticity is −2.0.

Here are a few own-price elasticities of demand published in 1969 by the National Food Survey Committee on the basis of statistics for 1962–7. They are, it must be emphasized, rough estimates rather than precise measures:

ESTIMATED PRICE ELASTICITIES OF DEMAND 1962–7

Beef and veal	—1.02
All carcase meat	—0.89
All meat (including poultry, bacon, chicken, tinned meat)	—0.45

It is evident that the more elasticity falls, in absolute terms, the broader is the category. If beef and veal get dearer, people can switch to pork or lamb, to poultry, bacon, chicken, tinned meat or to other sources of protein such as fish or cheese. But if we look at carcase meat together, the range of alternatives includes only rather different items. If, finally, we consider all meat as one, then the alternatives include only items which are very different. Hence it seems that the closeness of substitutes is a major factor determining the elasticity of demand. A price reduction will have a (proportionately) large effect if there are many other goods which meet similar needs and which have not fallen in price. Thus the own-price elasticities of demands for eggs, sugar and potatoes appear, in absolute terms, to be very small, while those for several individual green vegetables, whether fresh or tinned, come out greater than unity in absolute terms.

While the closeness and availability of substitute means of meeting the particular needs satisfied by any good is a prime determinant of the own-price elasticity of demand, it is not the only one. Substitution in a broader sense may also result from a price change. It may be, for example, that the growing relative cheapness of foreign holidays has attracted people's expenditure away from other things besides holidays in Britain. But the importance of such effects obviously depends on the satiability of wants. Thicker butter on one's bread will begin to seem unattractive rather sooner than longer or better foreign holidays will. So if butter and margarine were just as good substitutes as foreign and British holidays are, this satiability factor would make for a larger figure for the own-price elasticity of demand for foreign holidays than for that of butter.

1.3. *Income elasticity and price elasticity*

On the whole, it is to be expected that the more satiable wants are those met by goods on which the rich do not spend much more than the poor. In technical terms, a low income elasticity of demand for a good suggests that the wants which it meets are fairly limited. Income elasticity is defined as:

Proportional change in quantity

Proportional change in income

But this should not be taken to mean that butter (with an income elasticity of about 0.14) meets a less satiable want than margarine (with an income elasticity of around

−0.39). They both meet the same need. The suggestion is: (1) that there is a higher income elasticity for holidays in general than for yellow fats in general; (2) that this reflects a lesser satiability of wants for holidays, and (3) that this lesser satiability also leads to a higher absolute own-price elasticity of demand for holidays than for yellow fats.

All this, however, is no more than conjecture and cannot be proved. So if the reader does not find it plausible that one factor which makes for a high or low income elasticity of demand also makes for a high or low absolute own-price elasticity of demand, he is free to disagree. On the other hand, if he accepts the argument he must beware of the error of saying that a low income elasticity necessarily implies that the absolute own-price elasticity of demand is low. The reason why this would be wrong is that whether or not there are many close substitutes for the good in question also helps to determine its elasticity of demand.

Economic theorists have a completely different argument about the relationship between own-price elasticity and income elasticity of demand. The argument is one of almost pure logic, rather than being a supposition about the way people behave, like our satiability hypothesis. It runs as follows. If, other things being equal, the price of a good falls this will have two effects. One is the substitution effect; having become relatively cheaper there will be a shift in expenditure towards the good from substitutes. The other effect is the income effect; one price having fallen, and all other prices and income being unchanged, the total real purchasing power of those who buy the good has necessarily increased. Consequently, so the argument runs, there will be an income effect upon the amount of the good purchased. Hence the effect of a price change is composed of a substitution effect and an income effect.

Though perfectly logical, it is easy to exaggerate the practical significance of this argument, except for a few major items of expenditure such as housing and commuting. Apart from these two things, few single items in a household budget take more than 2% of expenditure. Thus a price change of 10% will usually alter real income by no more than 0.2%. If the income elasticity is as high as 2, the income effect will be no more than 0.4%. Consequently, if the own-price elasticity of demand is absolutely as low as −0.1, so that the 10% price change produces a 1% change in purchases, the income effect accounts for only 40% of the total effect. Yet this is an extreme case, combining an absolutely very low own-price elasticity of demand with a very high income elasticity.

If however attention is centred on a whole group of goods, such as clothing in general rather than, say, raincoats in particular, then matters are different. On the one hand, substitution possibilities are less, so that the substitution effect of a price change will be smaller. On the other hand, a 10% change in the price of all clothing will obviously mean a bigger change in real income than a change in the price of raincoats alone, so that the income effect will be larger. In the case of meat quoted earlier, we saw that the decline in substitution possibilities was the dominating factor, since the absolute own-price elasticity of demand was lower for the broader group. Perhaps this is related to the fact that the income elasticity of demand for all meat was estimated to be only 0.11 by the National Food Survey Committee and that the proportion of income spent on meat, according to the

Family Expenditure Survey for 1969, was 6.2% of total expenditure for the average household.

1.4. *Quality change – newspapers as an example*

It may now be useful to take a non-food example where quality changes mean that an explanation of what has been happening in terms of prices and incomes alone would be misleading. The example is that of national newspapers. Here are figures of average daily circulation, in millions:

AVERAGE DAILY CIRCULATION OF NATIONAL NEWSPAPERS

	1959 mn.	*1969* mn.
Dailies	16.1	14.6
Sundays	26.8	24.2

During this period the adult population rose and so did the standard of living, i.e. incomes after tax went up on average by more than the cost of living. On both these counts, therefore, an increase in newspaper purchases might have been expected unless, as seems highly improbable, it could be argued that newspapers were 'inferior' goods.

Newspaper prices, however, rose over the period by a great deal more than consumer prices in general. From 1959 to 1969, the cost of living index went up by over 40% whereas the prices of all the dailies doubled, except that both 'The Times' and the 'Guardian' went to 6d from 4d and 2d respectively. The Sundays, also, on average doubled in price. Since, other things being equal, a relative rise in price usually discourages purchases, it might seem that the price changes outweighed the growth of income and accounted for the decline in circulation. But it is always advisable to try to check whether other things really were equal. In this case they were not.

One reason was that the 'News Chronicle', 'Empire News', 'Sunday Dispatch' and 'Sunday Graphic' ceased to appear at the beginning of the sixties, that the 'Sunday Telegraph' first appeared in 1963 and that the 'Sunday Citizen/Reynolds News' came to an end a few years later. The circulation of those national Sunday news-papers that appeared throughout the period actually rose. Hence it might be argued that the fall in the total circulation of Sunday newspapers reflected the behaviour of newspaper proprietors rather than the behaviour of newspaper readers, many of whom, when deprived of their usual Sunday paper, bought another one instead.

No doubt there is something in this explanation; a narrowing of choice might be expected to reinforce a rise in prices (relative to other objects of expenditure) as a force contracting total purchases of a group of goods. However in the case of national daily newspapers it must have been a minor factor, since the circulation of the remaining newspapers continued to decline after the disappearance of the 'News Chronicle'.

The other factor which did not remain constant over the period was the size of newspapers. Quite apart from the introduction of colour supplements, most newspapers got bigger. Thus just from 1966 to 1969 there were increases in the average number of pages in all papers except for the 'Daily Herald/Sun' ranging from 45% for 'The Times' to 2% for the 'People'. Such increases can be looked at in two ways; as increases in quality or as

increases in quantity. In the first case, we keep to the copy
as the unit bought and say that though circulation (the
number of copies) fell, quality went up. In the second
case, we measure purchases in terms of the total number of
pages sold annually and obtain the following picture.
(The figures relate to thousands of millions of pages,
counting one page in a tabloid newspaper as equal to half
a page in a normal-sized paper.)

ANNUAL TOTAL PAGES SOLD OF NATIONAL NEWSPAPERS
in thousand millions

	1959	1969
Telegraph, The Times, Guardian, Observer	11.8	26.6
Mail, Sun, Expresses, Chronicle, Reynolds, Sunday Dispatch, Empire News	43.1	40.2
Mirrors, Sketch, People, News of the World, Sunday Graphic	33.6	43.5
Total	88.5	110.3

Looked at in this way, there has been a shift away from
'middlebrow' papers but purchases of newspapers have
not been declining in total; people, so to say, really
bought more newspaper in 1969 than in 1959. The rise in
population and in real income appear, after all, to have
had the expected effects, and the rise in the average price
per page was not large enough to offset them.

If there appears to be a paradox in all this it is easy to
dispel it. Although there is no direct statistical evidence
about how many households actually buy more than one
paper, we can deduce that the proportion has been
declining. National readership surveys show that there was
a marked fall in the amount of readership duplication
between newspapers. Thus the fall in circulation is
principally due to a reduction in multiple buying, and

has been smaller than the rise in the average number of pages per year. This was about a third for dailies and a fifth for Sunday papers.

It is natural to suppose that the reason some people were reading fewer newspapers in 1969 than in 1959 is that newspapers had become bigger. This cannot be proved or disproved, but it certainly looks as though it is an essential part of the answer. At any rate the point has been made that uncritical concentration on just number bought, prices and income may lead one astray in the analysis of consumer demand.

1.5. *Durable consumer goods*

The examples so far mentioned are all non-durable goods. The act of purchase is not completely synchronized with the act of consumption, since a little time may elapse between buying and using. During this intervening period the good exists as a stock in consumers' hands. But such stocks are not particularly important.

Things are different with durable consumer goods such as cars and furniture. These are not used up quickly, but yield a stream of services over a period of years. The stock of them held by consumers is a multiple of the amount bought annually, rather than a fraction as in the case of margarine and newspapers. This is one difference. Another is that hire purchase finance and bank loans are often used when durable goods are bought. Both of these differences introduce new complications into the analysis of consumer demand.

Consider first the influence upon the purchases of domestic refrigerators of the existing stock of them in people's houses. Given preferences, quality, advertising, availability, incomes and prices – all the factors listed above as relevant to the demand for non-durables – it seems reasonable to say that purchases will be smaller:

– the larger is the existing stock;
– the newer is the existing stock.

In other words, the more people there are who already have refrigerators, the fewer are the people who will buy them for the first time; and the more modern and trouble-free are the ones already installed, the fewer will be the people who will buy new ones to replace old ones. A large existing stock thus means that initial demand will be lower, and replacement demand higher, than if the existing stock were smaller. The faster refrigerators wear out, the greater the superiority of the current models over older ones, the greater will be the replacement demand corresponding to any given stock.

Although these propositions are fairly obvious, it is not easy to measure these effects. One set of reasons is purely statistical: there are no good figures either of purchases or of existing stocks in the hands of consumers. Consequently, any investigation into the factors determining purchases of consumer durables is as much a detective exercise in statistics as it is the application of economics. Since this book is not about statistics, the reader had better look elsewhere for an example. The last chapter of R. J. Nicholson's textbook 'Economic Statistics and Economic Problems' which discusses the demand for cars and TV sets will serve very well.

Margarine and butter are substitutes and one never catches a margarine firm urging its customers to buy butter. The relationship between Nicholson's book and this one is different; our books supplement each other instead of constituting alternative ways of ministering to the same need. Such a relationship is called 'complementarity'. Whereas a fall in the price of a substitute will lower purchases of a good, a fall in the price of a complement will raise them. The relationship, be it noted, lies in the capacity of the goods to meet consumer wants, not in any connection between their producers. (I do not even know Nicholson, but this does not alter the fact that a reduction in the price of his book would help rather than hinder the sales of this one and vice versa.) Other examples of complements are whisky and soda, sheets and blankets and electric appliances and electricity. In this latter case, most of the complications so far mentioned all apply at once. It is the stock of electrical appliances, not the purchases of new ones, which is relevant to the amount of electricity consumed by households. A fall in the price of electrical appliances relative to other heating and cooking appliances will, other things being equal, stimulate their purchase. This means an increase in the rate of growth of their stock and hence an increase in the rate of growth of domestic electricity consumption.

There is, it was suggested above, more than one reason why the analysis of the demand for durable goods is difficult. Besides the difficulty of getting statistics, there is the point that changes in government regulations controlling hire purchase have been fairly frequent and violent, often swamping such longer-term factors as changes in the size and age-structure of existing stocks. Thus even when there are good statistics, their interpretation is a complicated matter.

Chapter 2

DISTRIBUTORS' MARGINS ON
CONSUMER GOODS

2.1. *The nature of retail margins*

Retailers and wholesalers pass goods from the manufacturers to consumers and transmit orders and money in the opposite direction, from consumers to manufacturers. Naturally they charge for their services, and this charge sets a wedge between what the consumer pays and what the manufacturer receives. So, incidentally, does purchase tax, which is levied on wholesale prices.

The way in which the amount received by distributors is expressed varies between trades. In the case of furniture, for example, manufacturers rarely recommend retail prices, and their price lists state the normal prices they charge for furniture delivered to retailers. Purchase tax is included in these prices or stated separately and added. Retailers may sometimes obtain slightly lower prices when buying, in the shape of rebates for large purchases or for taking delivery at times convenient to the manufacturers, but these rebates are not particularly large. Retail prices are then determined by the retailers adding a mark-up. The standard figure is 55% on cabinet and upholstered furniture and 50% on kitchen and white-wood furniture. These are adhered to fairly widely; a sample survey carried out by the National Board for Prices and Incomes in 1968 found that over 70% of

31

multiple furniture shops' mark-ups and 60% of those applied by independent furniture retailers were at or near 55% and many of the others were at or near 50%. In other trades the dispersion of mark-ups is often much wider than this.

A mark-up of 50% can also be described (by looking at it from above instead of from below) as a discount of one-third on the retail selling price. Nowadays when, with few exceptions, manufacturers do not fix retail selling prices but merely recommend them, the discount is calculated in terms of a price which may not actually be charged! Thus take the case of a refrigerator with a recommended price, including purchase tax, of £50. If the retailer gets a standard discount of 20% on the recommended price net of purchase tax, and if the purchase tax is £5, he will pay 80% of £45 plus the purchase tax, i.e. £41. If he then sells at £49, his realized discount on the sale can be calculated to be 16.3% and his realized mark-up is correspondingly 19.5%.

The gross margin actually realized on the whole of a shop's sales is usually lower than its standard discount (if it is a trade which reckons in terms of discounts) or lower than the discount corresponding to its standard mark-up (if it is a trade which uses mark-ups). The reason is simply that some goods get spoiled, stolen, or sold at a reduced price.

2.2. *Differences in margins between products*

Variations in margins can be looked at between different goods in a shop, between shops in the same trade and between trades. By picking out a few examples of these variations we can gain some understanding of the factors which determine margins.

Consider, first, proprietary medicines. Those which are well established and heavily advertised have a large turn-over, are fairly easy to sell and will be readily stocked by retailers. The standard margin on such products as a percentage of retail selling price before tax is in the range 18%–25%. Unadvertised or slow-moving products on the other hand, have standard margins of 25%–33⅓%. Similarly, for most established and well-known products the wholesale discount is 12½% off the trade list price before tax, but discounts of up to 15% are allowed on less well-established products.

Another example which makes the same point relates to shoes. Higher mark-ups apply to expensive and fashion shoes, which involve the retailer in the risk of being left with unsaleable stocks, than to cheaper and more standard items such as men's shoes. Nationally advertised brands have lower mark-ups than others. Thus a National Board for Prices and Incomes survey in 1968 found the proportion of items sold at a percentage mark-up exceeding 55% (plus or minus 2½%) in a sample of multiple shoe shops varied as follows:

% OF CERTAIN ITEMS WITH MARK-UPS EXCEEDING 52.5%–57.5% IN MULTIPLE SHOE SHOPS, 1968

Expensive unbranded ladies' fashion shoes	43%
Cheap unbranded ladies' fashion shoes	24%
Expensive unbranded men's shoes	27%
Cheap unbranded men's shoes	28%
Low price nationally branded men's shoes	11%
Nationally branded sheepskin lined boots	8%
Nationally branded child's T-bar shoes	0%

2.3. *Differences in margins between shops*

Variations between shops in any one trade can obviously

arise because of a different mix of sales. If one shop sells a higher proportion of high-margin goods than another it will show a higher average margin. Apart from this, however, variation arises because costs vary according to the kind of service provided. The shopper really buys a good combined with retail service together in one transaction, and the share of the price which goes to the retailer will be greater the more service he provides. Soft carpets, convenient locations, credit, delivery, a large choice, numerous shop assistants and so on and so forth are all dimensions of good service and involve corresponding costs which have to be covered in the retailer's margin. Perhaps the reason furniture margins show less variation than margins on footwear and electrical appliances is that there is less scope for variation in the quality of services. All furniture shops provide free delivery and the majority of them put in a separate order to the manufacturer for each sale, making only a small proportion of sales from stock (which is why there are hardly any wholesalers in furniture).

Besides variation in the mix of products sold and differences in the amount of service provided to customers, there is a third reason for variations in the average gross realized margin within a trade. This is that some retailers may perform for themselves the functions of warehousing and physical distribution to their individual shops, together with all the paperwork which this involves. Other retailers have these services provided for them by wholesalers or by the manufacturers. It is, naturally, the smaller retailers who thus rely on others, while many of the larger retailers do their own wholesaling. Hence there is a difference in margins as a percentage of sales as, for example, Professor Reddaway found in his enquiry concerning the Selective Employment Tax. The 1967–8 percentage margins of the firms in his sample show this clearly:

1967–8 MARGINS OF LARGE AND SMALL RETAILERS IN CERTAIN TRADES

	Large Retailers	Small Retailers
Food	21.9%	20.9%
Confectioners/tobacconists/ newsagents	19.7%	16.6%
Clothing and footwear	34.3%	31.0%
Household goods	34.5%	30.0%

2.4. *Differences in margins between trades*

Finally, we come to variations between trades. Overleaf are figures for the average gross margins realized by multiples (excluding Co-ops) and by independents together, as shown in the 1966 Census of Distribution. Variety and department stores have been left out because they do a mix of business. Bakers have also been left out, because they combine manufacturing (baking) with retailing to an exceptionally high degree. In a separate column, figures for turnover per person engaged are given, counting two part-timers as one full-timer.

It is easy to think of particular reasons for particular variations. Food shops, for example, turn over their stocks much more rapidly than the kinds of shops higher up the list, which both reduces the costs of stocks and keeps down the amount of space required. But it is perhaps more useful to seek for some broad generalization which explains a good deal of the general pattern.

35

1966 MARGINS AND TURNOVER PER PERSON IN CERTAIN TRADES

	Gross Margin	Turnover per person
Boots and shoes	37.3%	£4,674
Radio and electrical (excluding hire and relay)	36.9%	£4,608
Men's and boys' wear	36.2%	£5,566
Jewellery, leather, sports goods	33.1%	£4,443
Furniture and allied	32.8%	£5,575
Chemists, photographic	30.3%	£5,085
Women's and girls' wear, household textiles, and general clothing	30.2%	£4,832
Cycle and perambulator	29.5%	£3,722
Hardware, china, wallpaper, paint	29.2%	£4,174
Bookshops, stationers	28.6%	£4,440
Fishmongers, poulterers	25.9%	£4,770
Dairymen	23.7%	£6,890
Greengrocers, fruiterers	22.6%	£4,314
Butchers	22.0%	£5,851
Off-licences	17.6%	£9,543
Grocers	16.1%	£6,676
Confectioners, tobacconists, newsagents	15.9%	£5,080

We start by saying that if different trades are, roughly speaking, equally profitable then differences in their gross margins reflect differences in the ratio:

$$\frac{\textbf{Cost}}{\textbf{Turnover}}$$

This can be written:

$$\frac{\textbf{Labour cost} + \textbf{Other costs}}{\textbf{Turnover per person} \times \textbf{No. of persons}}$$

and this can be expanded to:

36

$$\frac{(\text{No. of persons} \times \text{Earnings per person}) \times (1 + r)}{\text{Turnover per person} \times \text{No. of persons}}$$

where r is the ratio of Other costs to Labour costs.
Now 'No. of persons' is in both numerator and denominator, so cancels out. Earnings per person differ relatively little between trades. Hence the main sources of differences between trades lie in

– r, the ratio of Other costs to Labour costs;
– Turnover per person.

What is shown rather strikingly in the table is that Turnover per person varies relatively little between trades. It is high in off-licences because taxation makes drink so expensive. It is high in dairying because of milk which is delivered to the home. Much of the remaining variation can be explained by the so-called Gummer hypothesis which states that the time spent buying something is proportional to its price, has pretty well nothing to do with the nature of the good, and is inversely related to the frequency of purchase. There is, of course, a relationship between the time spent by the customer buying something and the time spent by the shop assistant selling it. Hence the Gummer hypothesis explains why a furniture salesman makes a few large sales in the same time as a butcher makes a large number of small sales. Behind the hypothesis there lurks the observation that people buy things particularly quickly when they know what they want before they enter the shop, and particularly slowly when a lot of money is involved. Gummer[1] is reported as saying that he would feel faintly improper if he went into a shop and bought a coat without trying

[1] The Official Secrets Act prevents me from disclosing whether Gummer is a person or a place.

on a selection and generally wasting time, even though the first one he tried on was the right colour and size and the one he eventually bought!

Looking back at this discussion of variations in retail margins it is apparent that most of them are explicable in terms of variations in the cost to the retailer and the effort required of him. For the present this is enough about retailing. Skipping lightly over wholesaling, we have thus found that the prices obtained by manufacturers equal the prices paid by consumers less a percentage. Though this percentage varies from case to case it varies explicably.

We can now go back to the demand analysis of the previous chapter and use the results of this chapter to shift over from demand at the retail level to demand at the producer level. The interesting point to note is that because margins are proportional (to price) rather than fixed in money terms, the elasticity of demand as experienced by producers is the same as that manifested by consumers. With a given percentage margin on any particular good, an $x\%$ change in the price charged by the producer means an $x\%$ change in the price paid by the consumer. Under these circumstances the definition:

Proportional change in quantity purchased
Proportional change in price

applied at the consumer and at the producer level gives the same answer. But, and this ought to be obvious, this does not mean that producers know what the elasticity of demand is for their product. Nor can one usefully criticize the analysis of this chapter, which rests upon 'other things being equal', by making the obvious point that once 'other things' change, margins will alter too.

Chapter 3

PRODUCER DEMAND

3.1. *The determinants of derived demand*

The purchases of producers are called inputs or intermediate goods and the demand for them is called a
derived demand. Thus the demand of margarine producers for fish and vegetable oils, and of newspaper
publishers for newsprint, are derived from the consumer
demands, less the distributors' margins, for margarine
and newspapers.

The volume of production is obviously the main factor
determing purchases of intermediate goods. Advertising,
selling effort and the number of selling points, on the
other hand, are of lesser importance than in the case of
consumer goods. The reason is simply that the buyer is
generally better informed and more expert about his
requirements. Such exceptions as farm tractors and office
furniture are fairly heavily advertised, but advertising
for other intermediate goods is generally rather less like
consumer advertising, being more informative and less
persuasive in style.

Besides the volume of production, the method of production is the other main determinant of a producer's purchases of intermediate goods. Thus brick purchases by
housebuilders go up either if the rate of housebuilding rises
or if the number of bricks used per house increases.

Changes of this latter sort, but in the opposite direction, have occurred owing to the greater use of alternative materials, particularly for interior walls where breeze blocks, hollow clay blocks and plasterboard are now often used instead of bricks.

Such substitution of one input for another can occur either because relative prices have changed or because technology has altered. In principle, this distinction between

- a cost-saving incentive to shift from one known method of production to another;
- the discovery of new methods of production;

is clear. In practice it is difficult to disentangle the two. Over recent years, for instance, the amount of plaster-board used in traditionally-built houses has risen considerably, so that nowadays it is used for virtually all joisted ceilings and for a large proportion of interior walls. The building trade has found skilled plasterers difficult to recruit and wet plaster, unlike plasterboard, requires time to dry. Furthermore, plasterboard's acoustic and other properties have been improved. These facts may explain the increase. Yet between 1954 and 1969, plasterboard prices scarcely rose, while many brick prices went up by almost half. It seems likely that this also helped the growth of plasterboard, even though British Plaster Board Ltd told the National Board for Prices and Incomes in 1969 that its *short-term* sales forecast would be the same whether or not a proposed 6% price increase was implemented.

Changes in the method of production induced by new discoveries or by price changes are not confined to such substitutions as fish oil for palm oil or plasterboard for bricks. The notion of substituting one input for another is more general than that. For example, it is possible to reduce the amount of newsprint wastage in newspaper production in a number of ways. This must be so, given that among ten newspapers examined in 1969 wastage rates varied from 4.4% to 12.2%. One cause of high wastage arises on stripping reels of newsprint when preparing them for use, and another occurs if an unnecessary number of turns is left unused on the reels. Better supervision and control can reduce both sorts of wastage, which means in effect that supervisory labour can be substituted for newsprint in the production of newspapers. Similarly, automatic tensioning devices can reduce the amount wasted through breakages, so that, in effect, automatic devices can also be substituted for newsprint.

3.2. *Substitution and output effects*

Input substitution, then, is a fairly general concept. It can be caused either by the application of new techniques or within a framework of existing techniques, by changes in the relative price of different inputs. The second of these, the substitution effect of a change in the price of an intermediate good, is not unlike the substitution effect of a change in the price of a consumer good. A rise in copper prices relative to aluminium induces a shift to aluminium core cables, so that the electricity supply industry can keep its costs as low as possible. A rise in the price of butter relative to margarine similarly induces some consumers to shift to margarine. The same effect would be produced by falls in the prices of aluminium and margarine. It is the essence of substitution effects that they are generated by changes in *relative* prices.

Since substitution effects occur in both producer and

consumer demands, it is natural to ask whether there is an income effect in both too. The answer is that there is something like an income effect in the case of producers' demands for input, but it is not quite the same and is therefore better called an output (or scale) effect in order to distinguish it.

Suppose that an input which accounts for 20% of a firm's costs rises in price by 10% and that there is no substitution effect. Then the firm's costs will be increased by 2%. If the firm simply absorbs the cost increase as a reduction in profit then there will be no output effect. If the increase pushes the firm into frantic activity to avoid the loss of profits by increasing sales, then the output effect will be positive. But if the 2% cost increase is simply passed on to its whole extent as a 2% increase in the firm's selling prices and if the average own-price elasticity of demand for the firm's products is, say, -1.5 then output will fall by 3% and so will purchases of the input which has risen in price. In this case, therefore, a 10% price increase diminishes purchases by 3% so that the elasticity of demand arising from the output effect is -0.3, which is 20% of the product's average own-price elasticity of demand.

This made-up example shows that the output effects of input price changes are likely to be very small, except when the input is a major one. Thus since, on average, the cost of plasterboard in a house is around £20, which is only a tiny fraction of the total cost, it seems safe to say that the output effect of a plasterboard price change must be pretty well zero.

The made-up example can be used to press home another point. It assumed a 20% increase in the price of some input, other things remaining unchanged (*ceteris paribus* as ancient Roman economists used to say). These other things include the demand for the product and the prices of other inputs. In a period of inflation these, however, will obviously not remain constant, but will go up too. Neither output nor substitution effect will then arise if they all increase proportionately.

3.3. *Demand for capital goods*

Inputs which are not used up in the production to which they contribute are called 'capital goods' and the expenditure upon them is called 'capital expenditure' or 'investment'. They are, of course, durable but it is better to avoid the term here. (Both bricks and concrete-mixers are durable in the physical sense, but for a housebuilder only the mixers are capital goods.)

The demand for capital goods on the part of producers can be looked at either as a stock or as a flow. In the first case we ask what determines the total concrete-mixing capacity, or whatever it is, which a firm aims to have. In the second case we ask what determines the rate at which new ones are purchased. The two are of course related. An increase in the target level of capacity relative to capacity currently owned will obviously step up the rate of new purchases.

3.4. *An example – farm tractors*

Consider, for example, farmers' demand for wheeled tractors which has been studied by A. J. Rayner (in 'Bulletin 113' of Manchester University's Department of Agricultural Economics) on the basis of annual statistics for the period 1948–65. He argued that high crop prices in relation to tractor prices made a larger tractor stock desirable by raising the value of the additions to output provided by extra tractors and other necessary inputs. This is an output effect. There was also, he asserted, a powerful substitution effect between tractors and labour so that a rise in agricultural wages relative to tractor prices also made a larger tractor stock desirable. He showed statistically that both these effects appeared to have existed. A rise in the desired stock relative to the actual stock led to an increase in the flow of tractor purchases so that, other things being equal, investment in tractors was lower the larger was the existing stock of tractors. Certain financial variables were also shown to affect the flow of investment, presumably because they helped determine the rate at which farmers could afford to acquire the additional tractors which it has become profitable for them to own.

Over the period studied by Rayner, the number of tractors owned by farmers more than doubled, while their input of hired labour fell by over a third. Yet the ratio of the average price of tractors to an index of agricultural labour earnings ended up little different in 1965 from its level in 1948. This makes it a little mysterious how there can have been a substitution effect. The answer is that, to put it crudely, tractors got better faster than they got more expensive, so that although the average price per tractor, like agricultural wages, nearly tripled, their 'real' price fell by around 16%. Similarly the improved quality of tractors meant that more than doubling in numbers involved a nearly fivefold increase in the 'real' stock of tractors.

As in other parts of this book it appears that an appreciation of the importance and extent of technical progress is essential if changes through time are to be understood. But while this is made clear by the facts in the last paragraph it is not obvious *how* Rayner estimated 'real' price changes i.e. how he corrected the increase in tractor prices by amounts which represented the quality improvement to obtain the 'real' change.

What constituted the improvement? Rayner's answer is as follows:

'Quantitative factors include an increase in average horse power of tractors sold from 24 h.p. in 1948 to approximately 50 h.p. in 1965 and an increase in the proportion of diesel engined tractors sold from less than 5% in 1948 to the total market by 1962. Qualitative changes are related to incorporation of hydraulics and p.t.o. systems into the standard models, sophistication of these systems (for example the features of independent p.t.o., automatic depth and draught control), the development of the differential lock, some form of gear change on the move and the provision of a much wider range of gears.'

The method used by Rayner for estimating what happened to the price of a constant-quality tractor, a method invented by Irma Adelman and Zvi Griliches, starts off with the set of list prices for all the main models in each of the years. The prices of all models are adjusted for attachments to get the prices for tractors equipped with self starter, p.t.o. and simple hydraulics. If, for example, the list price does not include hydraulics, the price of the hydraulics as an extra is added in.

Once these qualitative 'other things' have been made as equal as possible, a statistical regression analysis is then undertaken to find the relationship in each year between

45

the adjusted prices and such quantitative specifications as: belt horse power, diesel or petrol, maximum pounds pull, drawbar horse power, weight and fuel economy.

The final step is to choose a representative specification for the whole period of each of these items and to use the statistical relationship established for each year to calculate what would have been the list price of such a tractor in each year. Thus the process ends up with a price for each year of a tractor with a given set of attachments and with given quantitative specifications. This price series then provides an estimate of how the price of a representative constant-quality tractor would have moved over the period. As mentioned earlier, Rayner came out with a *reduction* of about 16% over the whole period 1948–65.

Chapter 4

COSTS

4.1. Cost differences between firms – cotton spinning as an example

It is an important feature of industry that there are frequently very considerable differences in costs between different firms producing similar products. In order to show this and to explain what sort of reasons may account for it, the case of cotton spinning will be taken as an example.

In 1969 the Textile Council published a large report 'Cotton and Allied Textiles' which included some detailed cost studies undertaken by the Shirley Institute. These included the following figures, relating to 1965–6, for four mills carding and ring-spinning cotton into yarn of approximately the same thickness (count group 32s). They are all expressed in (old) pence per pound weight of yarn.

COSTS IN PENCE PER POUND OF YARN AT FOUR MILLS:
1965–6

Firm no.	Labour costs	Overheads	Sales and General Admin.
1	6.6	4.0	1.2
2	8.5	3.9	1.6
3	9.2	3.6	0.9
4	11.1	4.9	1.9

Now these are not the only costs. The cost of the raw material is left out, since all mills buy in the same market, and depreciation is excluded from overheads because the amount set aside in the accounts is a very poor measure of the amount of capital used. Overheads as given are thus an agglomeration of rates, rents, insurance, power, heat, distribution, carriage, repairs and maintenance.

The first point to notice is that these unit costs differ quite a bit between the four mills. The second is that there is some tendency for the three groups of cost to vary in the same direction between mills.

Some of the overhead costs such as rates, being fixed as annual amounts, come out at less per pound of yarn the longer the hours worked per year. Mill 2 worked three shifts in both card room and ring room, mill 1 worked two and three shifts respectively, while mills 3 and 4 worked less than this in both card room and ring room. This explains some of the variation in overhead costs.

Lower labour costs do not stem from lower wages but from a better deployment of labour and a superior level of technology. As regards the first of these, the work loads of all of the operatives in mills 1 and 2, of half of them in mill 3 and of none in mill 4 had been determined on a work study basis. Furthermore, greater product standard-ization appears to lead to improved performance, though the figures available for these four mills do not enable this to be demonstrated. Apparently this is only partly a matter of such extra tasks directly involved in greater product variety as machine resetting. It is also due to the fact that continuous specialization enables attention to be concentrated on securing good performance standards in many minor aspects of the production process.

That the level of technology also affects labour costs is suggested by looking at the type of machinery used. Mills 3 and 4 had basically 1950-type machinery while mill 2 was more up to date. Mill 1 had a mixture, but the costs given above were based on the most modern part and labour costs in the older part were some 70% higher.

Most mills have a history of replacement and modernizations which leave them with a mixture of old and modern equipment. The influence of technical progress upon operating costs is thus difficult to discern. In order to get round this problem the Shirley Institute worked out figures of the 1968 operating costs of imaginary mills representing the best practice of 1950, 1960, and 1968. As before the figures are in old pence per pound and do not relate to all costs. This time they relate to 20s cotton.

COST AT 1968 PRICES IN PENCE PER POUND OF YARN AT NEW MILLS OF DIFFERENT VINTAGES

	1950 2 shift	1960 2 shift	1968 2 shift	1968 3 shift
Labour	7.0	4.7	3.4	3.6
Power	1.0	1.2	1.7	1.4
Waste	2.9	2.2	1.9	1.9

An explanation of the nature of the technical progress which secured these gains is outside the scope of this book. The point is that this progress is important and can create a fairly large difference in operating costs between mills equipped with machinery of different average ages.

In working out these figures, assumptions had to be made about the size of the mills. So far as operating costs are concerned, however, the assumptions were by no means crucial. Most of the machines employed in spinning are so small in capacity that many are used in one mill. A change in the size of the mill would merely mean installing more or fewer machines, all costing the same to operate (and to buy). The staffing and management costs of a mill may not vary proportionately with its size, however, though the size of mill which minimizes these costs per pound of yarn will be smaller for a mill with a wide variety of production than for one whose products are standardized.

4.2. *Cement as an example*

As a second example of the wide variation of costs within an industry, consider the 1966 average manufacturing cost of a ton of cement. This came to 75s 9d and as only 8% of it consisted of depreciation, the arbitrariness of this item does not matter much. Even if the six cement works with the most extreme costs are left out, the costs of the other thirty-six ranged up to 10s on each side of the average.

One important reason for this variation lay in works location, since the type of raw material used and accessibility varied from place to place, as did fuel costs. Thus the cost of coal varied between individual works by up to 30s per ton and the cost of oil varied nearly as much.

A second important reason for cost variation lay in differences in kiln sizes reflecting technological progress. Average kiln capacity rose from 95,000 tons a year in 1961 to 125,000 tons a year in 1966 (and there are now only two works with a capacity of under 200,000 tons a year). This change reflects the increase in the size of new kilns from 190,000 tons a year in 1961 to nearly 300,000 tons a year in 1966, and, it is expected, half a million or more tons a year in the seventies.

4.3. *Economies of scale*

One can, of course, say that there are economies of scale in cement production, in contrast with cotton spinning. In the seventies it would still be possible to build kilns of only 200,000 tons capacity and they would have higher unit costs than the larger sizes that will actually be chosen. Yet it is important to realise that, historically speaking, technical progress and the realization of scale economies are often one phenomenon, not two. Research and development was necessary in order to learn how to design and build the larger kilns. The same has been true in electricity generation, where set sizes have been getting larger. 500 MW sets should produce electricity more cheaply than 325 MW sets which in turn can produce electricity more cheaply than 120 MW sets. Yet at one time these 120 MW sets were the largest the manufacturers were able to build. They could see that future set sizes would increase but could not then actually build bigger ones. Various problems had to be solved for each subsequent upward step in size to be taken.

Economies of scale resulting from large plant sizes occur in a fair number of basic industries besides the two mentioned. These economies occur mainly in the initial capital cost and in labour cost; economies in raw material costs are less common.

Economies in initial capital cost can be expressed in terms of the exponent **b** in the formula:

Capital Cost = (A Constant Term) $\times$ **(Capacity)^b**

If $b = 1$, capital cost is simply proportional to capacity, while if b is less than one, capital cost rises less than proportionately to capacity, which is to say that there are economies of scale.

Two Americans, John Haldi and David Whitcomb, collected a lot of estimates of b and published their results in an article in 'The Journal of Political Economy' in 1967. They started with cost – size observations for 687 individual types of industrial plant and equipment. The figures they used were mainly collected from articles in engineering journals and were ultimately based on catalogues of industrial equipment. Of their 687 estimates of b:

42.2% were between 0.5 and 0.69;
90.0% were significantly below 1.0;
7.3% were not significantly different from 1.0;
2.7% were significantly above 1.0.

The reason that so few came out larger than one is that if big units are more expensive than small ones, firms will buy several small ones rather than one big one. In such cases the larger units are rarely made. The reason the great majority do show economies of scale is basically a geometric one: the amount of material required for tanks, furnaces, pipes, etc. depends to a considerable extent on their surface area and, as this is increased, the volume enclosed goes up more than proportionately. It is this which determines capacity.

Haldi and Whitcomb also presented estimates of b for whole plants. Most of the capital cost figures used to make these estimates come from engineering studies of a set of hypothetical plants, each producing the same product with the same technology available. The ratios of the smallest to the largest capacity lay mainly in the range between 4 and 20. The results are very similar to those given above. The median value for the scale-coefficient **b** is 0.73.

One reason for such economies of scale is, of course, that a larger plant requires larger individual items of equipment and that there are economies of scale for each of these separately. But there are other reasons too. Some pieces of equipment may be indivisible so that they are under-utilized in a small plant. Furthermore, some techniques may not be capable of application on a small scale.

4.4. *Airlines as an example*

Once we turn from the engineering of individual plants to look at all the costs of whole businesses, generalization ceases to be possible. In order to avoid a boring list of factors which may or may not actually be of importance in any particular set of circumstances, let us take the case of the airline industry. This was examined by the Edwards Committee in its report 'British Air Transport in the Seventies', since one of the issues they had to consider was whether economies of scale in this industry were big enough to justify a complete merger between BOAC and BEA.

The obvious way to start any such investigation, and one which the Committee followed, is to look for a number of firms which have much in common but which differ in size, and then to enquire whether there are any related cost differences. This, if one can afford it, is usually best done by going to the United States since Turvey's generalization (it does not rank as a law, exceptions having been discovered) asserts that at least seven of anything can be found there. At any rate the Committee found eleven US domestic airlines and ascertained that the four largest airlines had rather higher cost levels than some of the smaller airlines.

The Committee decided that four reasons in particular accounted for this. First, the big four faced more competition than the others, which meant a costly concentration on peak-hour operation and higher passenger service standards. Second, the big four's operations were more concentrated in big cities where the cost of ground facilities is particularly high and where air traffic delays raise operating costs. Third it was the big airlines which bore most of the burden of technological innovation. Finally, some of the larger airlines had a disproportionate number of short-haul routes.

These four points, however, as the Committee pointed out, are not so much related to the *scale* of operations as to their nature. Hence they went on to examine particular areas of airline operation where they thought that scale economies were likely to be found and came to the conclusion that the growth of an airline would lower its unit costs only if it operated one standard type of aircraft. In order to show the order of magnitude involved they constructed a table comparing the operating costs in £ per hour of two imaginary airlines engaged in short-haul operations, both using an identical aircraft costing £1.25 million.

This shows a 14% advantage in operating costs to the larger airline. As operating costs are about 70% of total costs, this gives Airline B an overall cost advantage of 10%.

The main reason why the larger airline has smaller depreciation though it pays no less for its aircraft is that

1969 OPERATING COSTS IN £ PER AIRCRAFT HOUR OF
TWO HYPOTHETICAL AIRLINES

	Airline A 5 aircraft	Airline B 50 aircraft
Depreciation (aircraft and spares)	60	50
Insurance	15	14
Flying operations	60	52
Maintenance	60	50
Station and Traffic	90	80
Total	285	246

its investment in airframe and engine spares need be only 15% of the value of its aircraft, as against 35% for airline A. It is indeed a common phenomenon that reserves against contingencies need to grow less than proportionately to size. The same spreading of reserves may enable the larger airline to secure better average aircraft utilization, say 2,600 hours a year rather than 2,400, creating some saving in respect of insurance as well as capital charges per flying hour. A third such advantage of large numbers ought to arise with respect to aircraft crews, who might do 650 hours a year rather than 600. This and lower training costs for the flying crews account for the scale economy in the Flying operations item.

Maintenance and overhaul costs ought, in the view of the Committee, to be lower for the larger fleet. They believe the reason that this does not show up in American cost comparisons is the diversity of tasks undertaken by the American airlines, which do not all have one standard type of aircraft.

On the whole, the Committee considered that the

advantages of scale in airline operation were less than
the economies to be obtained by specialization. They
instanced specialization on a few routes or specialization
on inclusive tours. Thus it is not surprising that they did
not recommend the amalgamation of BOAC and BEA.

4.5. *Depreciation and different cost concepts*

In this last case, but not in the earlier examples of this
chapter, depreciation has been included in the cost
comparisons. The point here is that both airlines would
pay the same price for the same aircraft, so that the higher
aircraft and spares utilization obtainable by the larger
airline implies a lower cost per aircraft hour. In other
cases, however, orthodox depreciation figures may be
misleading.

In order to discuss this, we need to raise the general
question of what we mean by 'Costs'. Economists have a
perfectly clear answer. They use the concept of 'opportunity costs', meaning that if doing x deprives one of the
opportunity of doing other things, then the best of those
other things is the relevant opportunity that was sacrificed
in order to do x. The value of that opportunity is the cost of
x. This cost concept really says that cost is the argument
against doing something. Since no one can deny that the
argument against doing something is relevant to the
decision of whether or not to do it, economists have a
pretty strong case for saying that their cost concept ought
to be used for decision taking!

When running costs are concerned, the economist is
unlikely to quarrel with the businessman. By and large,
if the businessman says that the labour, material and
power cost of making a whatsit is £0.99, the economist

will agree that he could save £0.99 by producing one less whatsit and will regard having the £0.99 as the sacrificed opportunity. Even here, there may be snags. The businessman may have worked out the figure of £0.99 by some rough and ready device which is rather inaccurate. Again, there might be argument when the price paid for materials has been changing, since there is then a choice between costing the material at the price that was paid for it when it was bought and costing it at the price paid now for what is bought to replace it.

Troubles of this sort are nothing, however, compared with the difficulties that arise in respect of joint costs and capital costs. Take the simple case of a taxi owner-driver who bought a new cab at the basic price of £1,365 in 1970 and expects to run it till 1977. What is the cost in 1972 corresponding to this? Here there are two quite different answers, the accountants' and the economists'. The orthodox accounting answer is that the cost consists of depreciation and interest. The first of these spreads the capital cost of £1,365 over the expected useful life of seven years according to some simple formula. (What is called 'straight-line' depreciation, the simplest, just takes one-seventh in each year.) The second item, interest, represents the interest that has to be paid, if the capital was borrowed, or which could have been earned if the owner-driver had the money and could have banked it somewhere instead of buying the taxi.

There are perfectly good reasons, as we shall see in a moment, for this procedure. But the economist neverthe-less takes a completely different line. To him, the cost before the taxi is actually bought is what will have to be paid to get it. This is a lump sum. Once the taxi has been bought, the economist regards its cost as the opportunity which is sacrificed by keeping it, i.e. the opportunity to realize its second-hand value. Hence the economist will regard the cost of having it in 1972 as the *excess* of its second-hand value at the beginning of that year over its value at the end. This is depreciation. Allowance has to be made for interest on the second-hand value too, since money at the beginning of a year can earn one more year's interest than money obtained a year later.

What if there is no second-hand market? Economists, being very logical, will say that if a firm has just spent a million pounds on a factory for which no one would offer a penny, then the cost of using it is zero. Yet a very large sum will be reckoned for depreciation and interest by an accountant.

The reason for the economists' approach is that they have developed concepts which are relevant for certain kinds of decision taking. Once this is spelt out, the rest is a matter of logic. Accountants, on the other hand, have to meet the requirements of company law and of the Inland Revenue. The protection of shareholders and creditors, on the one hand, and the need to determine a tax base on the other, both necessitate the calculation of the *annual* income of firms. Since their income, i.e. their profits, equals receipts less costs, this necessitates the calculation of *annual* costs. And this, in turn, means that amounts spent on acquiring things which last for more than a year, capital assets, must be spread over the number of years for which they are expected to last.

Now although the fundamental principle may be clear, coping with the thousand and one complications that arise in practice requires specialized skill. So most firms hire accountants. Once they are there, it is natural to try to use the results of their efforts for all sorts of things besides what they were designed for.

Accounting is, of course, not wholly devoted to ascertaining income. But a rather similar point applies to some other accounting tasks. Making sure that no one has stolen anything and checking on the performance of particular departments of a firm are two examples. Here too, accounting systems which were designed to do a particular job will do it perfectly well, while yielding figures which are less suitable in other contexts.

All this may explain why businesses often appear to use accounting figures in a way to which, so economic logic suggests, they are unsuited. They are available, they appear to be objective, they have been produced in a professionally respectable way, so why not use them?

There is more to it than this, however. There is also the ease with which the businessman can give one answer to two quite different questions:

- What will I save if I stop producing Model T? (i.e. what is the cost of Model T in the economists' sense?);
- How much shall I sell Model T for?

The single answer which *appears* to answer both questions is: The accounting cost of Model T. After all, since the business aims to get receipts from all its products taken together which will enable it to show a profit in the accounts, it appears reasonable to require a price on each product separately which is at least sufficient to cover its accounting cost.

The reader will notice that we have just switched from talking of one product produced over several years to talking of several products produced during one year. But there are joint costs in both cases, so the problems are fundamentally similar. Depreciation is an attempt to allocate the cost of a capital good between several years. The classical example of the other kind of jointness is the problem of how to allocate the cost of a sheep between the wool and mutton which it provides.

Jointness in costs, then, is an important problem. The economist claims that joint costs cannot be meaningfully allocated; the businessman, or his accountant, goes ahead and allocates them. Both are right! The economist uses 'allocation' in a causal sense while the businessman/accountant is deciding how to distribute the joint costs between different customers. If there is any error it lies in a pretence by the businessman/accountant that what he is doing is not a marketing decision but is something scientifically descriptive.

This book is about how the economy works. Consequently what concerns us is the behaviour of costs as seen by the people and firms who incur them. But some businessmen think like economists and others do not. Some accountants regard their figures as being relevant for almost any purpose, while others are perfectly well aware that different problems require different approaches. Thus in the analysis of actual economic behaviour the applied economist who is trying to explain, as distinct from the consultant whose task is to recommend, must beware of only using his own cost concepts. He may also need to understand the concepts used by the people involved. Occasionally he may simply find that some cost figures are not there at all!

An example of this occurred recently in the case of a brick company. Its accounting figures for individual brickworks showed operating costs (mainly wages) divided between such activities as setting, burning and drawing. But there was no information about how these costs would vary with changes in the kinds of bricks produced or with changes in output. While it seemed clear that these costs would all be escaped completely if the brickworks closed, dividing them by output to get a cost per brick for each activity did not give a good estimate of the effect of small output changes, as some of these costs were fixed with respect to such changes. Nor were there any standard costs, i.e. set material requirements and operational times which are multiplied by standard prices and hourly rates to get a cost figure useful for budgeting and price fixing. Thus the firm simply did not have the cost figures necessary for control purposes or those necessary for making the production plans which would minimize costs.

Chapter 5

COMPETITION

5.1. *Different kinds of competition*

The word 'competition' may denote either a process or a state of affairs. In the first sense, which is the business meaning of the word, it covers all of the activities designed to increase sales at the expense of some other firm or to avoid a loss of customers to other firms. There can be competition in purchasing too, but here we are concentrating on selling.

Competition as a state of affairs is a more academic concept, relating to the degree of freedom of manœuvre possessed by the firms in an industry. A 'perfectly competitive' industry is one where none of the firms can influence anything. They have to take prices as given and can achieve nothing by advertising or other forms of sales promotion. Each contributes so small a proportion of the industry's total production that, like one drop in the ocean, it has no perceptible influence upon the behaviour of the whole.

The nearest approach to perfect competition is to be found in agriculture, where there are thousands of farmers. Marketing Boards or governments often influence things, however, and in such cases the market is not perfectly competitive. But if we imagine an agricultural market which is totally free of such regulation it can be seen that the perfection of competition in the 'state of affairs' sense implies its absence in the 'process' sense. No farmer is competing with any other individual farmer in the way Procter and Gamble is competing with Lever Bros. Conversely, a detergent market dominated by two giants is not highly competitive in the state of affairs sense, but the process of competition is nevertheless very intense there.

Competition as a process can take several forms, and can well be intense even when price is not a major weapon in the competitive struggle. Prescription drugs, for instance, are chosen by the doctor, consumed by the patient and paid for by the National Health Service. Hence the price at which a new pharmaceutical product is launched will not have much effect on its success. Yet competition between the producers in developing new products is intense. So is competition in marketing existing products. It centres, as the Sainsbury Committee put it, 'on the various forms of sales promotion designed to inform, persuade or "remind" doctors of the merits of the products offered'. In 1965 some 14% of UK sales of National Health products was spent on sales promotion, nearly half of it on representatives, who call on doctors, at a cost to the companies which came out at about £250 per doctor per year.

5.2. *Free entry and its implications*

This chapter is about competition as a process under conditions of free entry to an industry. This means conditions under which new competitors have no permanent disadvantage relative to existing competitors.

As this is a negative condition it is best illustrated by its opposite, the existence of barriers to entry. Thus if the firms in the industry hold patents on some essential process and will not license the patents to new competitors, there is a very strong barrier to entry. If the existing firms own all the mineral deposits which are crucial, there is another barrier. A tariff on imports of the product constitutes a barrier to foreign entry. If the market is one for branded goods, and if enormous advertising expenditure would be necessary for any new competitor to get his product accepted by the buying public, there is a barrier to entry, though one that is surmountable by any firm with sufficient funds. Similarly, if economies of scale mean that a new firm would have to be large in order to be able to produce as cheaply as the existing firms, then there is a barrier to the entry of small firms, though not to large ones.

We now assert the proposition that the process of competition under conditions of free entry will prevent returns in an industry or trade from permanently exceeding earnings elsewhere. In the case of physical assets and capital funds these returns are purely monetary. The proposition states that people will go where the money is, in such cases where money is all that matters.

An apparent profit success for instant mashed potato has certainly stimulated new entry into that particular market. Yeoman and then Smash were the two brands which at one time had most of the market. But then the big retail chains started their own brands, importing from Canada, getting other food manufacturers to make it for them or even buying it from the makers of Yeoman and Smash, once they had installed their own plants, instead of importing from Canada. By 1970, the own-label brands of such firms as Sainsbury, Tesco, Fine Fare and of voluntary groups like Spar had around a quarter of the market. This case illustrates the point that new entry need not involve new firms and that the initiative can come from distributors as well as from manufacturers.

The proposition that competition when there is free entry will prevent the existence of persistently high returns has sometimes been extended to the labour market. Here it has been given the form that competition will equalize the 'net advantages' of different occupations when movement between them is freely possible. The trouble with this is that the non-monetary part of 'net advantages' can rarely be measured. Hence it is seldom possible to ascertain whether or not an observed difference in monetary returns is just offset by an opposite and equal difference in these non-monetary advantages. So this extension of the proposition is not often a useful one.

5.3. *Retailing as an example*

Retailing is one sphere where there is freedom of entry. People who run their own shops contribute both their own labour and their own capital, and their earnings consequently remunerate both. But if we reckon that independent retailers' labour should be valued at the average pay earned by branch managers of multiple shops in the same trade and with the same sort of turnover, then subtracting this from their total earnings gives a measure of the remuneration of their capital. The National Board for Prices and Incomes carried out a survey for three kinds of shops in 1968 which gave the following results:

TOTAL EARNINGS OF INDEPENDENT RETAILERS LESS IMPUTED WAGE, 1968

	Turnover Range in £000		
	0–20	20–50	50–100
Furniture	—£83	£588	£2,681
Electrical appliances	—£11	£498	£959
Footwear	£250	£348	£2,528

Since (i) there is a good deal of dispersion round the average, since (ii) the average for each turnover range differs between trades, since (iii) branch managers' earnings (which were subtracted from the total earnings of independent shopkeepers to give the above figures) may reflect age and career patterns and since (iv) capital requirements do not depend only upon turnover, it is pretty impressive that these figures do show some pattern. Higher turnover clearly requires more capital; more capital demands more remuneration and, the table shows, it gets it in all three trades. If it did not, the proposition about the effects of free entry would be refuted.

The table also shows that many independent shopkeepers in the smallest turnover class earn even less by combining their labour and capital in their own shops than they would earn if they had jobs managing other people's shops and lent out their capital to earn some interest. One possible reason for this is that the independent shopkeepers in the sample could not, in fact, have got jobs as managers. Alternatively, we could say that they valued independence very highly and that, counting this in, they were no worse off than paid managers owning an equal amount of capital. The figures obviously do not enable us to say whether either of these explanations is any good and, as pointed out above, it is difficult to see how the second one could ever be refuted or confirmed.

Consideration of the proposition that competition and free entry prevent abnormally high returns from persisting suggest an extension: Will free exit not prevent abnormally low returns from persisting? This is a difficult question. To answer it in this particular case we would need to know whether the large proportion of all these independent retailers whose total earnings fell short of comparable managers' earnings were likely to give up and go. Unfortunately there is no way of deciding this. There are in fact two good reasons why a trade may not shrink, even though a fair proportion of the people in it are doing very badly. One is that there may be a regular floating population of failures, with new optimists coming in just fast enough to replace the older ones who have finally had to give up. The other is the independence argument. Shopkeepers who are not making much money may nonetheless regard the amount as adequate to keep them in business.

The most obvious example of equalization of the returns of something in different uses is the shops themselves. A property owner with a shop to let will not care at all whether it is leased by a firm that sells radios or by one that sells shoes. The rent paid and the financial standing of the tenant are all that matter to him. Hence in any part of any shopping district there is a going rental value expected for shops which are to let and which is quite independent of the trade of the potential tenants.

This only applies to new leases. Rents have been rising in most shopping areas for many years. Hence a shop which was taken in 1960 will normally have a much lower rent payable under its lease than a similar shop next door whose lease was signed in 1970. Such differences can be quite significant. The survey quoted earlier in this chapter also involved, for a sub-sample of the shops, estimating their current rental value in 1968 on a standard lease and comparing it with the rents actually paid. For independent retailers in leasehold premises it turned out that 1968 rental values were, on average, *double* the actual payments. If all such retailers in the sub-sample had simultaneously had their leases renewed at 1968 rents, the proportion whose total earnings fell below the salary of a manager of a similar sized branch of a multiple would have risen from 31% to 48%.

5.4. *Impediments to adjustment*

This example shows that long-term contracts can impede the adjustment process by which extra high returns in any particular trade or industry are competed away by new entry. In fact long-term *anything* makes the adjustment process an imperfect one. The reason is that where:

- it take time to move resources into a use (e.g. to train labour),
- durable resources, once installed, are there for a long time (e.g. a purpose-built factory),
- short-term renting is impossible.

the monetary incentive to move resources into a particular line of business is *not* the returns being earned in it here and now. What matters is the *future prospect* of returns. In such cases, then, it is subjective and uncertain expectations that count, not currently measureable returns. So the proposition has to be watered down considerably. It now says that the process of competition under conditions of free entry will prevent returns from permanently exceeding earnings elsewhere, when entry necessitates a long-term commitment, *if* expectations turn out to be correct. Since the expectations held by firms are not usually made public this is not a proposition that can be tested. Furthermore, since the world is full of surprises we know that expectations often go wrong. In all such cases the proposition is irrelevant.

5.5. *The analysis of accounting data about profits*

Faced with this difficulty, economists have taken the apparently simple line of examining the pattern of profit rates as revealed by published accounting data to see what the facts are for firms in industry. An excellent example of such an investigation is that published by J. M. Samuels and D. J. Smyth in 'Economica', May 1968. It concentrates on the ratio:

$$\frac{\textbf{Profits net of interest and depreciation but before taxation}}{\textbf{Book value of net assets}}$$

and analyses figures for 186 UK companies over the period 1954–63. It looks at differences between industries only in terms of the concentration ratio in 1951. A concentration ratio is the percentage share of an industry's total production provided by the three largest firms in it and is assumed by economists to measure (inversely) the degree of competition *in the 'state of affairs' sense*.

One conclusion that Samuels and Smyth reach is that 'Firms operating in highly concentrated industries have less variable profit rates than firms operating in less highly concentrated industries'. This confirms what they call 'the theory' that 'although firms in the highly concentrated industries do not necessarily obtain higher-than-average profits, they are better able to withstand difficult trading periods because of their particular type of market in which they operate'.

This 'theory' is rather platitudinous, but the descriptive statistical result is well established. So is another: that 'Profit rates and firm size are inversely related'. This has a little more relevance to our free entry discussion. Large firms can do what small firms can do, but small firms are often not big enough to do what large firms do. Hence potential new entry into the fields occupied by small firms would seem greater than that into the fields occupied by large firms. So one might expect that there would be lower profit rates for the small firms, not higher ones as the authors found.

The trouble with this is that the profit/assets ratio has precious little to do with the *expected* rate of profit on *new* commitments, which, as argued above, is what free entry is about. Profits before depreciation involve some fairly arbitrary accounting conventions (which are not even standard between firms or accountants). Depreciation, as explained in the chapter on costs, is merely the result of a convention which is necessary for chopping up discontinuous time streams of outlays and receipts into years in order to produce an annual figure for income. The book value of net assets, finally, is even less meaningful. For companies which use a historical cost basis of accounting for fixed assets (the major component of net assets) it is the sum of capital expenditure over all past years less the amount of depreciation deducted to get net profits in all past years. Thus it is an extraordinary historical hodge-podge, reflecting the history of the company, the development of inflation and the wisdom of the Inland Revenue about the depreciation appropriate for tax purposes. For companies which value their assets on a replacement cost basis, on the other hand, it is an attempt to estimate what the figure would be if the general price level had never been lower in the past.

Since there is obviously not much to be said for the figures, one may ask why people appear to take them seriously. Samuels and Smyth are fairly frank about their deficiencies and basically rely on the argument that since they are the only figures available one might as well use them. This is indeed the common attitude. Most people prefer bad information to none at all. This is perfectly sensible, provided that one remembers just how bad it is. What is curious is that many businesses choose to rely on meaningless profit/asset ratios for checking up on their own branches or subsidiaries. Here, good information could be obtained, yet people have got so used to thinking in terms of bad information that they continue to want it!

5.6. *Bus companies as an example*

Occasionally better information is available to the outside enquirer too. In an article published in 'Economica', May 1969, for example, Professor Beesley and Janet Politi were able to measure the capital of bus companies in terms of the number of bus seats. Now the non-municipal bus industry provides four kinds of bus services:

Stage — short distance timetabled services with many stops.

Express   – long-distance timetabled services.
Excursions – ad hoc return journeys.
Contract   – the bus is hired and individual passengers
                make no separate payment.

The first two are controlled in detail by the Traffic
Commissioners, while Contract work is quite uncon-
trolled, except that no public advertising is allowed.
Hence entry into Stage and Express services is not free;
it is much easier into Excursion services and totally free
into Contract work. In consequence it is to be expected
that while profits per seat in the first two kinds of service
could exceed profits per seat in the controlled sector
without attracting a profit-reducing influx of competitive
services, the opposite would not happen.

The facts support this. In 1960–1, as the authors show,
profits per seat on both Stage and Express services were
higher than on Contract services. By 1965–6, Contract
work had expanded while total Stage journeys had fallen
by over 10%, reducing bus utilization and so reducing
revenue more than costs. Hence Stage services ceased to
be as much more profitable than Contract work. Express
journeys, on the other hand, rose nearly as much as the
number of Contract journeys and here the differential in
profits per seat was at least maintained.

We can usefully end this chapter by referring back to
Chapter 2 on distributors' margins. Near the end, it was
argued that if different trades were equally profitable then
the main sources of differences in margins between trades
lay in ratios of other costs to labour costs and in turnover
per person. This 'if' is now seen to follow, though only in a
very rough and ready way, from the fact that barriers to
entry into retailing are very few.

Chapter 6

EQUILIBRIUM, PRICES, DEMAND AND SUPPLY

6.1. *Equilibrium as an analytical device*

In an earlier chapter the approach via one thing at a time was introduced. It was explained that although other things rarely are equal, the unrealistic assumption that they are is nevertheless a useful aid to thought. We now come to the concept of equilibrium, a notion whose use ought to be viewed in the same way. The point about equilibrium is that whether or not it frequently exists in practice, the *assumption* that it exists is an aid to reasoning.

Equilibrium in a market is a state of affairs which is not subject to disruption by internal forces. It may involve no change at all, or it may involve steady growth or decline; in either case there is consistency between the plans and expectations of the buyers and of the sellers. Its opposite is disequilibrium. This exists, for example, if:

– some of the sellers are losing money and will eventually cease to supply;

– purchases continually exceed production, so that stocks in the hands of sellers are continually falling;

– orders continually exceed deliveries, so that unfilled orders are continually growing.

Economic theorists use the concept of equilibrium in a

market as follows. They first suppose an equilibrium to exist. They next assume some external factor to be different – we can take as an example the existence of purchase tax on the product. Then they work out what the equilibrium state of affairs would be under this alternative assumption. Finally they compare the two equilibria, regard the differences between them as the consequence of purchase tax, and say that this, that, and the other are the effects of purchase tax. If the two equilibria which are thus compared are stationary equilibria, as in most textbook theory, the approach is called 'Comparative Statics'. If the two equilibria are moving equilibria then the approach is called 'Comparative Dynamics'.

In either case, the approach is theoretical rather than empirical since equilibria can rarely be observed. Thus the use of comparative statics to answer the question of how a rise in car-workers' wages would affect the prices of new cars produces an 'if . . . then . . .' response. The 'ifs' are assumptions or statements about demand elasticity, car-manufacturers' policies, the relation of production costs to volume and so on and so forth. The 'then' is a deduction about how the prices of cars in two market equilibria would differ with car-workers' wages higher in one than in the other.

6.2. *Empirical approaches*

There are obviously other ways of answering the question about how a rise in car-workers' wages will affect car prices. One is to ask some top men in British Leyland, Ford and Vauxhall. The other, which is more work but unavoidable if one never meets the top men, is to see what happened in the past and *assume* that the pattern of behaviour thus revealed will continue to operate in the future.

Now finding out what happened in the past is easy if one can find an occasion when a large change occurred in car-workers' wages, during a period when everything else that one can think of stayed unchanged. But this hardly ever happens, and an econometric analysis using highbrow statistical techniques may be necessary to disentangle all the other things that were not equal. Such techniques more often than not run into difficulties, however, so that no sure answer can be obtained from them. One reason for this is that some of the necessary statistical information may not exist or, if it does, may have various snags. The other reason is that there are real obstacles to inferring cause and effect from an observed past. If car-workers' wages, to take the simplest possible case, always went up or down when steel prices went up and down, it is absolutely impossible to distinguish the effects of wages from those of steel prices.

These two reasons why statistical inference is normally difficult and frequently impossible are of tremendous importance to the applied economist. Nevertheless, they are not the subject of this book, so let us proceed.

Equilibrium analysis and the study of the past, we have argued, are two ways of answering questions about the workings of a market. Actually, they answer slightly different questions. In a historical analysis, we think of all the factors which *may* have influenced, say, the proportion of UK motor cycle production that was exported. We then find out (if all the statistical problems vanish) which of these factors did exert an effect, how strong it was and how long it took. Thus part of the answer provided is of a 'what happened next' variety.

Equilibrium analysis, on the other hand, is about how things would have been different under hypothetical alternative circumstances. Textbook demand and supply theory is comparative statics. Moreover, it is equilibrium theory related to particularly simple situations, that is to say situations where advertising, product innovation and other important phenomena do not matter. The circumstances where it can be applied most readily are to markets for standardized commodities where there are many sellers and buyers, many transactions and good communications.

6.3. *The importance of factors other than price*

In many other markets it can be very misleading to think about prices in isolation. Producers often have a marketing strategy about what they are aiming to sell and how they are aiming to sell it. Design, packaging, distribution, promotion and prices are all parts of one co-ordinated effort.

The point that price is often only one of the factors relating demand and supply does not only apply to manufactured goods. Consider, for example, the market for building society mortgages where 'price' means the rate of interest. A building society which cannot provide all the mortgages that are sought from it has at least the following six alternatives to increasing the interest rate charged as a means of restricting demand:

– excluding certain categories of houses, such as pre-1920 dwellings or non-traditional houses;

76

- making less generous valuations or lending a lower proportion of its own valuations;
- requiring borrowers to have been depositors or shareholders;
- reducing the maximum amount it will lend in relation to a borrower's income;
- lowering the maximum term of the mortgages it will grant;
- increasing the delays which applicants suffer.

The example is a simple one, but makes the point. It also illustrates the difficulty of obtaining statistical data which was mentioned above. Statistics of building societies' mortgage lending rates are available but no systematic information is collected about variations in the six non-price variables just listed. So any attempt to study the demand and supply for mortgages must start with a significant handicap.

6.4 *The complexity of prices*

Another general point to be made about prices is that they are fairly complicated. Thus the price list for plaster-board covers four basic products: wallboard, baseboard, lath and plank. Prices are different for insulating and for plain board and depend on thickness. They also depend upon order size, being lowest for large orders. They include delivery and in this respect are unusually simple, since they are uniform for the whole country except the Scottish Highlands. Discounts from these list prices are allowed to merchants, through whom BPB deals.

A Sheffield engineering firm provides an example of a

firm which has no price list. Its products have no standard dimensions, each customer having his own special designs for items which he incorporates in his own products. The staff of the engineering firm have to quote prices for an average of one hundred different sorts and sizes of items per working day. Less than half of these quotations result in orders, competition being keen.

In its report on Metal Containers, published in 1970, the Monopolies Commission gave details of the Metal Box Company's price structure for standard-size processed food cans. There are ten of them, each available in eight combinations of tin coating specification and finish, which gave eighty prices to start with. There were then extra charges for decoration. The resulting prices were subject to a complicated system of discounts and rebates (some of which the Monopolies Commission disapproved of) related to total quantities purchased, and to quantities of each size separately, to off-season deliveries and, for customers under an exclusive buying agreement, to total purchases of food and beverage cans together. However the largest customers, who between them provided over half of Metal Box's sales, all bought at special prices or on individually negotiated terms.

These two examples show that price structures are complicated. Hence except where all list and negotiated prices change by exactly the same proportion, while all discounts and rebates stay at unaltered percentages, price changes are likely to be complicated too, and a statement that a firm's prices went up by an average of 6% may conceal a great deal of detail.

Bearing this in mind, let us consider two cases of price determination. Both of them relate to intermediate products where the buyers are expert in assessing their requirements and in judging product quality. Sales promotion activities are therefore much less important than with most consumer goods and the role of price in determining sales is correspondingly greater.

6.5. *Pricing policy of the Metal Box Company*

The first case is that of the Metal Box Company, which has a near-monopoly of the sales of the kind of tin cans which are used for tinned food and drink, though some large users make their own. This firm told the Monopolies Commission that in determining its prices it aimed at obtaining an overall profit of 10% on all sales. Its basic list prices, though not changed annually with the costings, were based on standard costs, and the discount structure was designed to reflect economies of scale in supplying its large customers. Thus for five out of six standard sizes quoted by way of illustration, the margin of standard cost below list price was 17%–19%. In the six years 1963–8 profits varied between 10.2% and 12.1% of sales of the kind of tin cans in question, total costs including various items not included in the standard works costings. This average of about 12% fits in with the overall average of 10%, since the rest of the company's business was less profitable, there being more competition!

Though its prices have thus been generally determined in relation to standard costs, market considerations have occasionally played a role. In the late 1950s the company made successive price reductions on beer cans to promote their sales in competition with glass bottles. In 1958, when a competitor started up, it reduced prices and in a few cases it negotiated special terms with customers specifically to avoid loss of their business to the competitor. On the other hand in 1969, when orders ran ahead of its budgeted forecasts, it met the demand by means of overtime working at an increase in cost, without raising prices more than $5\frac{3}{4}\%$. This increase, however, appears to be wholly explained by a rise in tinplate prices and in other costs.

Here then, we have the case of a firm with a near-monopoly of sales, but with some large users making their own cans and with its own customers able to do so too. Its prices were based on standard costs and were intended to provide a target rate of return on sales. They were occasionally modified for competitive reasons, but were not increased because orders pressed upon capacity, and were altered relatively seldom.

6.6. *Pricing in cotton spinning*

The second case is the spinning of cotton, man-made fibres and mixtures – an industry already discussed at the beginning of Chapter 4. Its yarn prices over the period 1966–9 were looked at by the National Board for Prices and Incomes, which concentrated upon conversion margins (or 'value-added' in economics jargon). These subtract the current costs of raw material from the yarn prices agreed at the time for delivery a few months ahead.

Conversion margins fell in the latter part of 1966 and during most of 1967, going down to 90%–95% of the May–December 1966 level for cotton and mixture yarns, and down to 87% in the case of spun viscose yarn. In 1967 yarn production was well below the 1966 level. At the end of 1967, in some cases, and much more noticeably after mid-1968, conversion margins rose. By the autumn of 1969 they were in the range 110%–118% of the May–December 1966 level, except that mixture yarn margins were at 131%. This rise apparently reflected an increase in orders and, after mid-1968, some limitations on yarn output capacity. These were due to a loss of labour, since output had not got back to the 1966 level. Spinners' order books were fairly full, however.

Some sixty firms were engaged in the spinning industry during this period. The variety of yarns is very great, however, and each mill specializes in particular types or thicknesses of yarn. Thus the choice of mills for any particular weaver or knitter may be much more limited than the number of firms would suggest. Most weavers and knitters do not deal with more than two or three spinners and undertake a change of supplier only reluctantly. Price competition is therefore less intense than a superficial inspection would suggest. Nevertheless, it is pretty clear that conversion margins first went down and then went up, when orders first rose and then fell. This, together with the negotiation of a separate price on each contract, affords a fairly sharp contrast with the case of tin cans.

6.7. *The variability of pricing policy between industries*

That different patterns of pricing behaviour are to be found in different industries can be shown more generally. Consider the answers of 553 large businesses to a simple postal questionnaire as described in a British Institute of Management information summary (no. 148). They were asked: 'On what basis do you generally fix your prices:

Cost plus
Cost plus modified by market conditions
Market conditions
Other?'

The percentage ticking each, in the same order, was:

$$10\%$$
$$59\%$$
$$26\%$$
$$3\%$$

The two examples and the questionnaire responses make it clear that pricing behaviour does differ, so that the question 'How do firms fix prices?' does not have one answer. Clearly, most prices reflect cost changes in some way or other. Most are also influenced by market pressures, whether from competitors or from the relationship between the flow of orders on the one hand and capacity on the other. But how can we go farther than this and explain what will happen when? Can we find a link between (i) the structure of the industry and the nature of its products on the one hand and (ii) the forms that competition takes and the relative importance of costs and of market conditions in price determination on the other hand?

The answer, alas, is that we cannot establish such a link. Armchair economic theorists can construct plausible hypothetical relationships, but there is precious little in the way of empirical investigation in this country. It is just a bit too easy to set out an elegant theory and then to suggest rather pompously that the task of testing it is left for other (lesser) mortals.

6.8. *The difficulties of empirical studies*

One way of attempting to describe, rather than to explain, pricing behaviour is, as mentioned earlier, the statistical study of the past. The difficulties which this involves are amply illustrated by the article 'The roles of labour productivity and demand in the pricing process: An inter-industry study using time-series data' by Anthony J. Phipps in the November 1969 'Bulletin of the Oxford University Institute of Statistics'. His analysis is confined to the four 'broad sectors of industry' which are relevant and for which data are available. The main snags which emerge are that:

- the sectors are so broad (Timber, Chemicals, Paper and Textiles) that the variety of behaviour within each of them must be very great;
- a trend value of labour productivity multiplied by average hourly earnings is the best available statistical approximation to the movement of standard labour costs in each broad sector;
- the best available indicator of demand pressure in each broad sector is the relationship of (i) current output to (ii) the highest level output has previously reached multiplied by a compound growth factor relevant to the sector. Figures for unfilled orders and stocks are just not available;
- the behaviour of foreign competitors who export to Britain is not brought into the picture.

Phipps' conclusion is that 'where actual labour costs provide the better explanation of changes in wholesale prices, demand is of some importance in the pricing process whereas, in those industries where price movements conform more to the trend in labour costs, demand is of little or no importance'. In the light of the problems listed, Phipps is surely right to speak of this as 'very tentative'. Yet most other British studies are even less revealing since they deal with manufacturing as a whole.

6.9. *More about factors other than price*

All we can say, then, about the effects in a particular market of an upswing in the volume of orders or of actual purchases, is that these effects *may* include price increases. Economists believe that these are more likely when there are many firms competing than when they are few. The other possible effects, which may either accompany the price increases or take place in their stead are:

- longer delivery delays;
- a drawing down of stocks;
- a reduction in sales promotion efforts;
- deterioration in the quality of the goods or of the accompanying services.

It will be noticed that these effects are listed in a certain order. Price changes are the easiest to measure and quality change is the most difficult – at least so far as the outside observer or government statistician is concerned. Actually, as explained earlier, prices are very complicated and so even their measurement is not that simple. A temporary discount here and a reduced delivery charge there can easily fail to show up in a price index. Some American authors have demonstrated that industrial prices in the United States are a good deal more flexible than shows up in list-price changes and in official price indices. The same is probably true in Britain.

Changes in the qualities of goods, or of the accompanying services, have just been mentioned as a short-term phenomenon. But they change not only as a short-term response to alterations in market conditions. They also change in the longer term, as the discussion of farm tractors in Chapter 3 showed. Since such phenomena easily escape ordinary price statistics, 'real' increases in prices can be overstated. Hence another example of long-term quality improvement may serve to hammer home their importance. It comes from Ever Ready, whose price increases in 1970 were reported on by the National Board for Prices and Incomes. For three lighting batteries the effective price, expressed in pence per hour of discharge life, changed as follows:

COST TO PURCHASER OF THREE BATTERIES MEASURED IN PENCE PER HOUR OF DISCHARGE LIFE		
Battery	1950–2	1969
A	2.8	2.1
B	1.2	0.9
C	0.7	0.5

Shelf life was also increased. Thus for battery A, the lighting discharge after twelve months storage tripled over the ten years ending in 1969. These improvements were fairly gradual, while prices were fairly stable up to 1967. Hence the 'real' prices, despite appearances, fell fairly steadily over this period.

The point that in many markets a rise in price is only one possible reaction to an upswing in demand applies with particular force to the labour market. If wages were an important part of the mechanism for adjusting the supply of labour in particular industries or occupations to the demand, we would expect this to show up in the statistics. We would, that is to say, expect relative wages to rise in rapidly expanding industries and to fall in contracting ones. By and large, however, this does not happen; changing wage differentials seem to play a very small part in inter-industry labour movements.

85

Falling stocks and lengthening order books cannot go on for ever. Consequently the list of possible longer term reactions to an upswing in demand must exclude these temporary reactions. We are left with:

- quality decline;
- reduced sales promotion;
- price increase;
- output increase.

The last of these meets the increase in demand, while the first three serve to choke it off by discouraging would-be purchasers. It is an important proposition in economics that *one or more of them will occur in response to an increase in demand* unless

- *either* the increase is temporary
- *or* some kind of quantity rationing is introduced.

Older readers will recognize the truth of this proposition by remembering the War. Output and prices of civilian goods were kept down, rationing was widespread (both official and unofficial) and shopkeepers had to make no effort to sell what they had.

6.10. *The supply curve and its elasticity*

There is a good deal of theory which ignores stocks, unfilled orders, quality changes and sales promotion and thus supposes price and output changes to be the only possible reactions to demand changes. This is the theory of the supply schedule (curve) and the related concept of the elasticity of supply. The latter is defined as:

$$\frac{\textbf{Proportional change in quantity}}{\textbf{Proportional change in price}}$$

86

i.e. just like the own-price elasticity of demand, except that here 'quantity' is quantity supplied and this elasticity is normally positive.

The notion of a supply curve and of its elasticity is meaningful in markets where sellers respond to prices rather than determine them themselves. Unfortunately, despite the simplicity of such markets, measurement of supply relationships is trickier than the measurement of demand relationships – at least as regards those of non-durable goods. The time factor is the reason for this contrast. Margarine purchasers can alter their behaviour pretty fast in response to price changes. Wheat farmers, on the other hand, decide how much they sow rather than how much they harvest, and do so in relation to the prices that they expect to rule for the harvested crop. Thus wheat supply is a matter of their decisions and of their expectations, whereas the statistics available usually relate to actual harvests and to realized prices. Furthermore, a sustained expectation of higher prices may lead farmers to acquire more equipment over a period of years, so that the full response of supply to price is spread out over time. In technical jargon, the elasticity of supply may be greater in the long run than in the short run.

Supply, then, both of goods and even more of labour, is less promising than demand for empirical illustration or for application. Since this is an empirically oriented book, we had better leave it there for the present.

6.11. *Prices, information and incentive*

It is a fundamental proposition of demand and supply that an increasing scarcity of something leads to the substitution for it of other things. Where the 'something' can be bought and sold, we have said that a major manifestation of growing scarcity is a rise in price relative to the prices of other things. Such a rise in relative price provides an incentive:

- to purchasers, to substitute other things;
- to sellers, to increase supply.

As was mentioned earlier, a large part of economic theory has been built on the assumption that prices are the only mechanism which adjust demand and supply to each other. This, it has now been made clear, is a gross simplification in many markets. Nonetheless, it is a useful simplification, so long as one remembers that it is only part of the story. It is important to understand that price changes simultaneously provide both a message and an incentive to buyers and sellers in a simple way. Theories that explain how this happens have to ignore other information channels and other incentives in order to set out a clear and rigorous account of the working of a price mechanism. These other things are ignored, in other words, for expository reasons. Simplification is the ordinary scientific procedure of concentrating on one thing at a time because it is too difficult to think about everything at once.

Since this book is about applied economics it does not attempt to expound the pure theory of a price mechanism – that is left to the standard textbooks. Purchasers, as we have seen, can get information not only through impersonal market prices but also:

- by discussion with suppliers;
- by reading newspapers and journals;
- through trade associations;
- from consultants;

and in many other ways. Similarly, purchasers can derive an incentive to economize in the use of something not only by a rise in its price but also for example:

- from longer delivery delays;
- from poorer service or a deterioration in quality.

Similar remarks apply to sellers. In particular, most large firms put a considerable effort into forecasting the demand for their products. This involves information-gathering by all sorts of means, including market research. Indeed information is something which is bought and sold (and which is often provided free or at a subsidized price by governments).

The importance of all these non-price factors varies from one market to another. Demand and supply are often mediated by price but it is a great mistake to *assume* that an analysis running only in terms of price will fit any particular case. Both incentives and the provision of information need to be investigated.

Chapter 7

DEMAND AND SUPPLY IN LABOUR MARKETS

A general account of how labour markets work would require a whole book. The aim of this chapter is much more limited. Its purpose is to show, by example, how economic analysis can be used to explain some observed phenomena. First, there is a case study of low pay. Then, two occupations where wage relativities reflect market conditions in an obvious way are briefly considered. Finally, there is an example of an occupation where, in contrast, earnings do not serve to adjust demand and supply and where quality variations appear to play an important role.

7.1. *Low paid workers*

Laundry and dry cleaning is an industry whose workers are low paid and an industry which is declining. It is natural to suspect a connection between these two facts. But first, let us elaborate them a little.

The National Board for Prices and Incomes carried out a sample survey of pay and conditions of employment in the industry in September 1970. The figures obtained can be compared with figures from a national survey covering all industries made in the following month (see opposite).

Hours of work were practically the same. There was, of course, considerable variation around these averages.

FULL-TIME WORKERS' AVERAGE GROSS WEEKLY WAGE
EARNINGS, SEPT.–OCT. 1970

	All manual workers	All unskilled manual workers	Laundry and dry cleaning
Men	£28.5	£24.8	£21.7
Women	£14.3	£14.2	£11.3

Thus 10% of all male manual workers earned £18.3 or less. As many as 29% of the full-time men workers in the laundry and dry cleaning industry were in the same bracket.

The industry (except for linen hire) has been declining since at least 1965. The growth of washing-machine ownership, the spread of launderettes, improved soaps and detergents, together with greater use of easy-care fabrics are no doubt the main causes. At any rate, the labour force fell by 24% between 1966 and 1969.

The trouble with the idea that low pay and decline are linked is that the industry has been a low paying one for a long time. It is, in fact, traditionally a low paying industry and the tradition appears to be a good deal older than the decline. Average hourly earnings can be compared with hourly earnings in industry over fifteen years and appear to have been about a fifth below them for most of the period, though it may be true that the gap is a little wider than it used to be.

Some other explanation must therefore be sought for the low level of pay in this industry. The characteristics of its workers seem relevant. To start with, it is important to notice that not very much is demanded of them. Apart from pressing and one or two other tasks, the bulk of the work requires neither training nor experience. Some concentration and dexterity is needed, but that is fairly

91

usual, and the work, with few exceptions, is not hard. Thus many jobs are sufficiently undemanding for the industry to be able to employ disabled and mentally handicapped people to good effect.

The characteristics of the labour force, as ascertained by social survey carried out by the National Board for Prices and Incomes, fit the requirements of the industry. On the whole, workers' educational attainments were low and a high proportion of them regarded their state of health as impaired or as creating employment difficulties. About 40% of them gave the nature of their job as a reason for choosing it, but a quarter of the men said their present job was the only one open to them. The great majority of all workers had had previous jobs, mostly including work in other industries, and redundancy had been the most common reason for leaving the last job – at least among the full-time workers. In the case of part-time workers, getting married or looking after the family was the main reason.

These factors appear to explain why, on average, laundry and dry cleaning workers are ready to accept low wages (or unable to obtain better wages elsewhere). If they do, then it might be expected that those of them whose earnings are much below average should display these characteristics to an extra degree. This, in fact, appears to be the case, at least in the case of the full-time men workers. The proportion among them of the elderly, the disabled, the poor in health and of those who had lost an earlier job or found their present one the only one available were all higher.

A third of all laundry workers surveyed lived within half a mile of their work. At least for many of the women, working close to home is an attraction, but of course a desire or need to do this limits the range of jobs open to them. Thus this point really confirms the argument.

Finally, it is a feature of the industry that its rate of labour turnover is higher than the national average. This is largely due to a large number of young people entering and leaving soon, so that there is a constantly floating group of young workers. Thus it seems to rely for the younger part of its labour force upon a constant procession of people who try out a job in it and then try something else. Perhaps what it offers to them is the ready availability of a job.

7.2. *Wage relativities within a trade*

The influence of supply and demand upon the relative earnings of people doing the same job in different places or under different conditions is best seen in occupations where there is little collective bargaining. One such occupation is contract cleaning – mainly of offices – where most of the work is done by part-time women workers. Many of them are married, and have children and stay in a job for relatively short periods. The employers determine pay and conditions, but have to pitch them at levels which will secure the requisite number of workers. The relations between employers and workers, besides being mainly at a workplace level, are thus fairly casual. In such conditions one would expect the pattern of earnings to reflect relative scarcity and workers' preferences fairly closely.

Over half the cleaners are paid on a 'job and finish basis' but the employers determine the amounts in the light of the time the jobs should take. Hence hourly rates of pay can be used to obtain an indication of pay patterns.

A National Board for Prices and Incomes survey found the average hourly rate for part-time women cleaners to be 31p in 1970. This was practically the same as recorded for cleaners and charwomen in all industry in the Department of Employment's New Earnings Survey. Thus contract cleaners on average earned about the same as cleaners who were directly employed.

Regional variations were large, earnings per hour ranging from 36p in London to 24p in Scotland. However there were finer variations within a region and even within a town. Such factors as travel distance and cost, pleasantness of the area and the kind of cleaning to be done all had a part. Early morning shifts, being much less popular for working, were paid on average 35p per hour as against 29p for early evening shifts.

Average hourly earnings for part-time women cleaners were lowest, and nominal hours per week were highest, in Scotland. In regions where hourly earnings were higher, hours were shorter – except for London. This curious inverse relationship arose from the fact that once a cleaner earned more than £4 a week, the incidence of National Insurance contribution and of the Selective Employment Tax raised labour costs by 30%. Hence the cleaning contractors made every endeavour to keep hours and rates low enough to stay within the £4 limit. In London, however, the average hourly rate of 36p would only allow an average 11.1 hours within the limit and most London cleaners want more work than this. Consequently the £4 barrier had been broken by two-thirds of the London cleaners as against only a fifth in the rest of the country. This explains why London cleaners formed an exception to the inverse relationship observable elsewhere.

Another labour market where collective bargaining is largely absent and where pay appears to respond flexibly to changes in demand and supply conditions is the market for secretaries and shorthand typists. Office staff employment agencies play a very important role here, both by placing girls in jobs, for a fee paid by the employer, and by providing temporary staff.

The National Board for Prices and Incomes obtained a good deal of information in 1968 relating to the work of these agencies in London. It appears that applicants seeking jobs through them are much rarer in the summer months than in the spring or autumn. In addition, employers need to replace staff who are on holiday. The resulting shortage in summer is met partly by the employment of temporary staff – mainly for periods of six weeks or less. Thus it was estimated that some fourteen and a half thousand temporary secretaries and shorthand typists were employed in Greater London at the end of July 1968 as compared with only eight thousand the previous December.

On the supply side, a survey conducted by the Alfred Marks Bureau in 1968 showed that a large proportion of temporaries are unable or unwilling to take permanent jobs. The reasons were various, including family commitments, an impending change of residence and a preference for the more varied routines of temporary work. However there were some who were waiting for a permanent job.

These facts lead one to expect that pay would be higher in the summer than in winter and that the earnings of temporary staff would not get far out of line with the earnings of permanent staff. Both expectations are confirmed.

95

AVERAGE HOURLY WAGE RATES PAID BY AGENCIES TO
TEMPORARY SECRETARIES AND SHORTHAND TYPISTS BY
LARGE AGENCIES – CENTRAL LONDON

Date	s	d
1.12.64	7	10
31. 7.65	9	9
1.12.65	8	5
31. 7.66	10	2
1.12.66	9	1
31. 7.67	10	4
1.12.67	9	9
31. 7.68	10	11

Although the general trend was steeply rising, there was
a fall from each July to the following December. The
rates charged by agencies were, of course, higher but
showed the same general pattern.

At the end of July 1968, temporary secretaries and
shorthand typists earned about two shillings an hour more
than permanent staff. Most of them, however, received
no payment during absence through sickness and only a
few were eligible for paid holidays. The difference thus
roughly matched the difference in fringe benefits.

Like the preceding example, we have a case where
many of the workers have some freedom in deciding how
long they work. It may seem that workers in industry,
whose earnings and conditions are regulated by collective
agreements, have less choice. Studies of overtime working
carried out by the National Board for Prices and Incomes
show, however, that a surprisingly large number of
industrial manual workers can, in fact, choose (within
limits) how much overtime they work. A survey of
employers produced the result that, for 81% of their

workers, overtime is voluntary and that the trade unions rarely oppose it in practice. Furthermore, it even appears that some workers choose to work less than the standard week. The proportion of adult male full-time workers who lost pay through voluntary absence, sickness, late arrival or early finish was distinctly higher for those doing no overtime at all than for those doing more than two hours' overtime!

More overtime is done by those men whom one would expect to want to increase their earnings: younger married men and those with lower hourly earnings. All in all, therefore, many male manual workers do appear to have and to exercise choice between how long they work and how much they earn.

7.3. *University teachers*

We now turn, for contrast, to an occupation where earnings play a relatively small role in adjusting supply and demand. Universities have national uniform salary scales, with the exceptions of Oxford and Cambridge and of teachers of clinical medicine. (In what follows teachers of medicine are not considered.) For lecturers, senior lecturers and readers there are incremental salary scales. In the case of professors there is a range, but the average for all professors in each university must not exceed a stated level.

It follows from this that the ability of universities to pay teachers of different subjects differently is very limited. They can appoint them to different points in the salary scale and they can give them a more or less senior rank. However, not more than 35% in each university may be in grades above lecturer and in any case the grades are few. Some professors, finally, can be paid a higher than average salary, provided that others receive less than this.

If teachers (medicine apart) are divided into four groups: Humanities, Pure Science, Applied Science and Social Studies, it appears that teachers in the last two groups are, relatively speaking, scarcer than in Humanities and Pure Science. We shall now provide some evidence for this and then discuss the way in which this different relative scarcity manifests itself. The facts and arguments that follow are all based on a study sponsored by the National Board for Prices and Incomes and carried out by the Higher Education Research Unit at the London School of Economics. The work on pay was the particular responsibility of David Metcalf.

Over the years 1960/1 to 1969/70, universities expanded a great deal. The proportion of staff in Applied Science did not change much, while the proportion in Social Studies rose a great deal. The absolute increase in staff numbers was thus greatest in the latter category.

A survey of job applications made to a sample of universities in 1968/9, when the rate of recruitment had slowed down as compared with previous years, provides some information about recruitment problems.

RECRUITMENT AT 21 UNIVERSITIES, 1968–9

Subject group and no. of subjects	Applications per vacancy	Extreme difficulty in appointing lecturers	No difficulty in appointing lecturers
Humanities 3	24.8	6.4%	34.9%
Pure Science 3	11.6	1.6%	42.9%
Applied Science 2	4.7	16.7%	0.0%
Social Studies 4	10.4	20.2%	13.1%

A comparison of average basic salary by grade of a 10% sample of university teachers appears to show that teachers of Applied Science do get more, but fails to show the same for teachers in Social Studies:

AVERAGE BASIC SALARIES, 1969, £

Subject Group	Professors	Lecturers
Humanities	4,511	2,147
Pure Science	4,689	2,191
Applied Science	4,707	2,424
Social Studies	4,423	2,188

Salaries, however, are very much age-related. It seems that perceptions of fairness make the age of a teacher a major factor determining his appropriate salary, and a long history of incremental salary scales both reflects and reinforces this attitude. Hence a better way of seeing whether the greater scarcity of teachers in Applied Science and Social Studies is reflected in salaries – within the limited scope described above – is to compare salaries by age group. It turns out that Social Studies staff have a higher basic salary than in Pure Science or Humanities up to the early forties. After that, they fall behind. Applied Science teachers, however, have a higher basic salary at nearly all ages.

These differences, however, are not large. On the other hand, basic salaries are supplemented by other earnings. Those of these other earnings which come from outside universities are presumably more related to grade than to age. In the case of professors, whose supplementary earnings are on average more than double the supplementary earnings at other grades, those in Social Studies and Applied Science do obtain much more than those in other subjects. However, there is a far greater dispersion round the average in the case of supplementary earnings than in the case of basic salary. Many teachers in all subject groups merely earn a little in the way of various fees; large non-academic outside earnings are obtained by a small proportion of teachers.

It could be argued that a greater readiness on the part of universities to permit scarce varieties of teacher to obtain non-academic supplementary earnings is an alternative to paying them a larger amount for the same work. As yet, however, there is no evidence that the teachers who do more outside work do correspondingly less teaching, research and administration in their universities. Perhaps they are just energetic people who do more work of all kinds! In any case, while universities may well allow statisticians, say, to obtain more outside earnings than historians, it does not follow that this is a device intended to give them a higher total income. Historians might well be granted permission more often if only they asked for it.

What matters, if money is important, is not the earnings of university statisticians versus the earnings of university historians. For each speciality, earnings as a university teacher (plus the non-monetary advantages of being one) versus earnings in some *other* job (plus its non-monetary advantages) must be relevant. Thus if universities were using salaries and supplementary earning possibilities to attract enough recruits and stem losses, a comparison between subject groups within universities might not show it. The point is that recruitment in 1968/9 was more difficult in Applied Science and Social Studies *even though* basic salaries were higher than in Humanities and Applied Science for the younger teachers. Thus some other mechanism had to cope with this difference which was not solved by earnings, and that something was probably a differentiation of quality between the two pairs of subject groups in recruiting.

The evidence of such a quality differential is confined to measurable phenomena. These are probably less important than the personal and intangible characteristics of recruits which impress (or depress) an Appointments committee. Nevertheless they point in the expected direction. The proportion of successful applicants for lectureships who were under twenty-five was higher in the two 'shortage' subject groups than in Humanities and Pure Science and the proportion of all teachers with a first or upper-second was lower.

While there is no evidence about how new recruits regarded their earnings prospects in university life in comparison with other jobs, there is some information on this score about university teachers in general. A sample of teachers was asked whether by comparison with the 'single most likely other occupation' the 'conditions offered by the academic profession are, better, about the same, or worse' in a number of various respects. We can see how many thought that they were financially worse in universities, i.e. the teachers who thought they might earn more elsewhere.

Clearly, most university teachers in the last three groups feel they could earn a larger salary elsewhere, though most would not expect to earn more on the side as well. Presumably the reason why more Science and Social Studies teachers do not leave is that they value university life. All the same, the percentage of staff making applications for non-university jobs during 1968/9 was two to three times as high among these teachers as among

% OF TEACHERS CONSIDERING ACADEMIC CONDITIONS AS
WORSE THAN IN MOST LIKELY OTHER OCCUPATION

	Starting salary	Long-term salary prospects	Opportunity for supplementary earnings
Humanities	32	37	23
Pure Science	60	57	18
Applied Science	57	66	15
Social Studies	45	57	18

teachers in the Humanities. Thus to the extent that universities use monetary incentives to keep the staff they have got, one would expect the differentiation to be between Humanities on the one hand and the three other subject groups on the other. To the extent, however, that academic equality is considered important one would expect to find little of what teachers in the Humanities would call 'discrimination' against them. The figures suggest that while younger teachers in the Humanities do earn less than their opposite numbers, their senior colleagues do not. Perhaps academic status confers academic economic power!

Chapter 8

THE RELATIVE PRICES OF
DIFFERENT MANUFACTURED GOODS

8.1. *The importance of material and labour costs*

This chapter is about the analysis of long-term changes in relative prices in the manufacturing sector. In the space of one or two years, different industries, as we saw earlier, react differently to these changes in demand which involve big changes in the degree of capacity utilization. But over longer periods it is changes in costs that dominate relative price changes. This does not mean that demand is irrelevant. Demand affects costs by affecting the growth of output and this, as we shall see, is very relevant to cost changes. All we are saying here is that we are now looking at trends in prices rather than at short-term fluctuations in them. In this context we disregard such changes as result from different short-term reactions to an upswing or downswing in sales volume.

For manufacturing industry in general, gross output (the aggregate value of goods made and other work done) in 1968 according to the Census of Production consisted of:

- 60% cost of goods and work done purchased from other firms;
- 40% payment for certain services and value added to materials by the process of production, half of this being wages and salaries.

On average, therefore, 60% of the price of manufactured goods was made up of purchases of fuel and materials and another 20% went in wages and salaries.

It follows from this that we can get quite a long way in explaining long-term changes in the relative prices of different manufactured goods by looking at trends in:

- the prices paid for materials and fuel;
- wage and salary levels;
- the efficiency with which materials, fuel and labour are used.

In practice, trend movements in wage and salary levels differ astonishingly little between industries. Differentials in earnings, in other words, are very persistent, a phenomenon which is found in other countries too. As a rough and ready rule, therefore, wages and salaries enter into explanations of relative price changes only via differences between industries in their share of gross output. An equal percentage rise across the board in earnings will directly raise costs more in labour-intensive industries than in industries where labour costs form a small part of the total.

The influence of materials and fuel costs is more varied. From 1963 to 1970 the prices of basic materials and fuels used in manufacturing rose by 26% and the wholesale prices of manufactured goods rose by 29%. For textiles, however, the figures were 4% and 17%. Presumably the smaller rise in the prices of materials and fuel used in textile manufacturing is a major part of the explanation of the smaller rise in output prices.

The textile price index is calculated using about seven hundred price quotations. A comparison of each of these with the relevant input price changes would be more interesting but is, unfortunately, impossible. Indices are published for the output prices of some much narrower categories of goods than textiles in general, but there are no corresponding indices of input prices. It is possible, however, to pick out some prices which rose much more or much less than the overall average of 29% and attribute the difference to price changes of particular major inputs. For example imported raw jute prices rose by 50%–60%, jute yarn rose by 56% and jute piece goods rose by 47%. Similarly, imported aluminium ingots rose by 44% over the same period, 1963–70, and rolled and extracted aluminium products went up in price by 42%. Conversely, the prices of imported raw wool fell heavily and worsted yarn prices remained almost constant.

8.2. *Changes in efficiency*

Although, as these examples show, changes in the prices of materials and fuel are often an obvious cause of changes in output prices, there remain some important changes where a different explanation is needed. This is particularly obvious in the cases of the many chemicals, plastics and domestic electrical appliances whose wholesale prices rose by less than 10% from 1963 to 1970. Given the general level of increases, these small absolute increases meant a *relative fall* of around 20% in the prices of these particular groups of products. In contrast with worsted yarn, there is here no major raw material whose price has been declining. Thus there is a presumption that the third factor listed above was at work. But why should efficiency in the use of materials, fuel and labour have been rising especially fast in particular industries? Perhaps it is related to exceptionally fast growth of output.

An increase in efficiency in an industry is an increase in

its output accompanying a fall or constancy in all inputs. The substitution of, say, machinery for labour in response to a rise in the price of labour relative to that of machines will raise output per man. But as this is achieved by using more machinery, it is different from an increase in efficiency. Using less labour without using more machinery, or, better still, using less of both, is an increase in efficiency.

Technical progress and economies of scale are the two prime sources of increases in efficiency. As we saw in Chapter 4, they are easier to separate in principle than in practice. But for present purposes this does not matter too much. Neither of them can usually exert much effect save through increased capital expenditure. The application of new techniques generally demands some re-equipment of existing factories or even the building of new ones. Economies of scale are realized by the construction of large new plants. Hence while the progress of technology differs from one industry to another and while the scope for economies of scale varies between industries, what is true for nearly all of them is that the degree of *realization* of these potential increases in efficiency – cost reductions – depends upon the pace at which new plant and equipment supplement or replace existing plant and equipment.

We have reached the conclusion, then, that, apart from differential changes in materials and fuel prices, those industries whose prices fall in relative terms will be those where:

- technical progress and/or economies of scale are above average;
- capital expenditure is particularly high in relation to the existing stock of plant and equipment.

The trouble with this sort of proposition is that, in order to see how well it works, we need to try it out on a large number of industries. However interesting it may be in other contexts, a blow by blow account of the evolution of one particular industry cannot explain changes in its product prices relative to others. We need statistics to test the argument and we do not have them.

8.3. *Changes in output and in labour productivity*

The best we can do is to look at the relationship, across a large number of industries, between the growth of:

- labour productivity;
- output.

The first of these, as already pointed out, may reflect a substitution of capital for labour rather than increased efficiency. The second of these, on the other hand, is not the only factor determining capital expenditure in relation to the existing stock of plant and equipment. A long life of plant and equipment, for example, will keep down the proportion of the existing plant and equipment which is replaced in any year. Nonetheless it remains true that the faster output grows, the more will capacity have to expand and the larger will capital expenditure be. So a positive correlation across industries between the rate of growth of output and that of output per man employed cannot *prove* that the argument is right. But it helps.

The matter was investigated by the late Dr Arthur Salter in his important book 'Productivity and Technical Change'. The second edition of this contains some additional material contributed by Professor Reddaway. Diagram 2 combines their work. It relates to twenty-seven

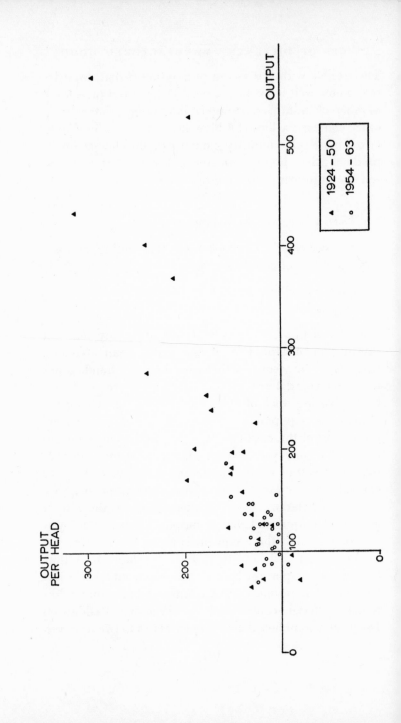

PER HEAD

300

200

100

0

100

200

300

400

500

▲ 1924 – 50
○ 1954 – 63

manufacturing industries over the period 1924–50 and to a partly different collection of twenty-seven industries over the period 1954–63. Using mainly Census of Production data they calculated a change in output and a change in output per person employed for each of these industries. Their results as plotted show a clear tendency for changes in output per head to be positively related to changes in output. Thus the argument is supported, though not conclusively demonstrated.

8.4. *The identification problem*

Returning to the more general proposition, it is important to notice a potent source of confusion. We can observe that, for example, the production of synthetic resins and plastic materials rose very steeply in the sixties and that an index of their prices actually fell. What has been said above leads us to suspect that heavy capital expenditure was involved, that technology was changing rapidly and that the scale of new plants rose over the period. Suppose that we are right. Then we must ask whether what we observe was:

- an extension of demand, stimulated by a fall in price which reflected a fall in costs due to technological progress and the exploitation of economies of scale;
- a response of costs to an increase in output called forth by a growth in demand which was stimulated by factors outside the industry;
- or a mixture of the two.

The facts as given above do not enable us to tell. Additional information is required in order for us to identify the respective roles of supply and demand in the sequence of observed changes in prices and outputs.

This 'identification problem' occurs frequently in economics. Indeed we skimmed over another example earlier in this chapter. When a product price rises in association with a large rise in the price of the main raw material used to manufacture it, there are three possible explanations:

- changes in the supply of the material, or in other demands for it, force up its price, so raising the cost of producing the manufactured good;
- a growth in demand for the manufactured good raises the desired demand for the raw material so that its price is bid up;
- a mixture of the two.

Knowledge of the industry in question going beyond statistics is necessary to sort this out.

Chapter 9

THE VALUE OF TIME AND THE
RELATIVE PRICE OF SERVICES

9.1. *The increasing scarcity of time*

It is a fact of British economic history since the war that, in material terms, the standard of living has risen a great deal. The amount of goods that can be bought in exchange for the average earnings from a week's work has gone up very considerably. What is more, the working week has shortened for some workers, though not for manual workers (where growing overtime has offset much of the reduction in the nominal working week). It seems, however, that the rise in people's purchasing power over goods has been proportionately much greater than the rise in the amount of non-working time.

Now goods take time to buy, to use and to look after. So what we have just said means that the time required to spend, enjoy and maintain the fruit of a week's earnings has gone up proportionately more than the number of hours left over for *not* working. The demand for time has risen relatively to the supply – so time has become scarcer.

9.2. *The rising price of services*

Time, of course, cannot be sold. The millionaire cannot purchase an hour from a beggar in order to experience a twenty-five hour day. Rich people can hire poor people to do things which will save their time, but as we *all* get richer it does not necessarily happen that more of us buy more direct services instead of doing things ourselves. One reason that this may not happen is that many services grow relatively more expensive. This too follows from the first paragraph of this chapter. The rise in the purchasing power of earnings means that the ratio:

$$\frac{\text{price of labour}}{\text{price of goods}}$$

has risen very considerably, wages having gone up relatively to the price of goods. Hence the higher is the labour content of anything we buy, the greater (other things being equal) will be the increase in its relative price through time. Since many services are very labour-intensive this means that they have risen in price relative to most goods. By the end of 1970, for example, the retail price index for domestic help, hairdressing, shoe repairing, laundry and dry cleaning had risen by about 60% since the beginning of 1962 as compared with an average rise in the wholesale prices of all manufactured products of only 35%. This last increase would have been a little bigger had not raw materials gone up slightly less in price but the contrast is still striking.

Retailing is also a fairly labour-intensive service, so we should similarly expect its 'price' to have risen relatively to the manufacturers' prices of the goods themselves. This means we expect that, as time passes, the share of expenditure in the shops that is kept by retailers will rise. It implies, in other words, an increase in the realized gross retail margin and this is exactly what has happened in most trades over the long run. In successive Censuses of Distribution the average for all retailing has altered as follows:

AVERAGE GROSS MARGIN FOR ALL RETAILING	
1950	22.2%
1957	23.3%
1961	24.9%
1966	26.7%

If anything, these figures understate the effect, since with self-service and with more pre-packing by manufacturers, the amount of service provided per unit of sales has fallen in some kinds of shops.

9.3. *Technical progress and relative wages as complicating factors*

Our conclusions are, then, that time has grown scarcer and that services have grown relatively more expensive. These are both central features of our recent (and prospective) economic growth.

These conclusions, though empirically correct, do not follow with remorseless logic. Technical progress has been left out of the argument. If new developments had:

– made consumption activities less time-consuming,
– raised labour productivity in services faster than elsewhere,

to a sufficient extent, then the conclusions would have been wrong. But although examples of time-saving innovations (drip-dry shirts) are easy to find, their total effect has not been strong enough to offset the extra demand for time resulting from the huge increase in output. In fact most services have not got cheaper. (As

Professor Baumol once said, a half-hour horn quintet takes two and a half man hours to perform 'and any attempt to increase productivity here is likely to be viewed with concern by critics and audience alike'!)

There is another link which has been left out of the argument but which, in practice, does not destroy it. If rates of pay had risen much more slowly in labour-intensive trades than elsewhere, services might not have risen in price relative to goods. In fact, however, this has not happened. Taking April 1960 as 100, average weekly earnings of men manual workers in laundries, dry cleaners, garages and shoe repair were 164 in October 1968 and 159 in all manufacturing industries. For hourly earnings the corresponding figures were 173 and 165. Full-time women manual workers showed an even closer correspondence in the rise in earnings. (In both cases the level was lower in these service trades than in manufacturing.)

9.4. *Substitution and other effects in the demand for services*

The gradual rise in the prices of most services relative to the prices of most goods exerts a substitution effect upon the demand for services. Taken by itself, therefore, the relative price change can be expected to reduce the purchase of services. Cutting down on maintenance, using a washing machine instead of a laundry and buying a record instead of going to a concert are three examples. However some of the other things that have also been changing can work in the opposite direction. Let us look at them one by one.

First, there is the rise in real incomes. Average earnings now will (i) buy a lot more goods than before and (ii) where productivity has been increased, more services too. (i) is the proposition we started with, but (ii) is less familiar. In order to see its meaning, let us show that where productivity has *not* increased, the power of the average income to buy that service has not increased either. Suppose that a barber can produce no more haircuts in a day now than he could fifty years ago. Suppose too that barbers' earnings have risen in the same proportion as average earnings. Then, tax complications apart, the 'haircut value' of average earnings will be unchanged.

The point is, then, that an average income will buy more of *most* goods and of some services than it used to do. Average real income has risen and this will raise the demand for everything except inferior goods (and, if there are any, inferior services). So the income effect generally goes in the opposite direction to the substitution effect.

While goods in general are substitutes for services in general, particular goods may require service, so that the income effect which increases purchases of these goods will carry with it increased purchases of these complementary services. While the shift from using a carriage to using a car depended upon technical progress, it is a growth of income which turns one-car families into two-car families, and two-car families require more garage services. Similarly the rise in the ownership of television sets involves an increased demand for the services of TV repairmen.

A second factor which may modify the working of the relative price substitution effect is technical progress. Since this takes many forms, no generalization about its effects on the demand for services as a whole can be made. Here are a few examples, however:

- a car generates more of a demand for garage repair services than a horse did for blacksmith services;
- the invention of first the safety razor and then of the electric razor destroyed the demand for barbers' shaving services;
- the development of pain-killing injections has done a lot for dentistry.

9.5. *Interaction with the growing scarcity of time*

Thirdly, while services are becoming relatively dearer, time is becoming relatively scarcer. The net effect of this may be to stimulate the demand for time-saving services. But the growing scarcity of time will more generally increase the time intensity of consumption. Staffan Burenstam Linder, whose book 'The Harried Leisure Class' is the source of much of the analysis in this chapter, provides some good examples:

- wasting food instead of using up leftovers;
- driving at a higher speed in a more expensive car;
- owning both a camera and a fishing rod, but using each only half as much as when only one could be afforded;
- abandoning cultural pursuits which, like reading, do not involve much consumption in favour of others which do.

The growing scarcity of time may help to explain why, as countries grow materially richer, people do not appear to feel correspondingly better off. Since Britain is poorer than the United States it may also explain the kernel of truth in the remark that while Americans spend money to save time, the British are prepared to spend time in order to save money! In fact, of course, both are prepared to spend money to save time and the real point is that, being richer, Americans are prepared to spend *more*.

How do we find out how much people are prepared to spend in order to save time? One way is to examine the choices made by car owners between commuting to work by car and by public transport. Those who choose to drive are adopting a more expensive but quicker journey, while those who choose public transport are saving money but taking more time. Thus comparison of the time and cost of the alternative chosen with the time and cost of the rejected alternative for a commuter can give us an upper or lower limit for the value he or she places upon time. If a commuter saves ten pence by going to work by bus, taking fifteen minutes longer about it, then the value per hour must be less than forty pence.

QUARMBY'S ESTIMATES OF THE VALUE OF COMMUTERS' TIME, LEEDS 1966

Average hourly income	Value of Time
7s 2d	1s 9d
10s 6d	2s 7d
14s 9d	answer not statistically reliable
23s 0d	4s 10d

This argument is only valid if other things are equal. They clearly are not. But questionnaires can find out about these other things too and a statistical technique known as discriminant analysis can be used to sort out their influence. A paper by David Quarmby in 'The Journal of Transport Economics and Policy' for September 1967 describes an investigation he made in Leeds in 1966. His analysis, using five other variables as well as time and cost, gave the results (see page 117) in shillings and pence for the four income groups into which his sample of commuters was divided.

It does indeed appear that those who are better off attach a higher value to time, which supports the earlier analysis in this chapter.

Chapter 10

THE RELATIVE PRICE OF URBAN SPACE

Central urban space, like time, becomes scarcer as a consequence of economic growth. The result is that there has to be a substitution of other inputs for urban space. In those parts of the urban property market where rents and prices are free to rise, incentives to achieve this substitution are provided by the upward movement in them which results from the growing scarcity.

10.1. *Scarcity and office rents*

Office rents are not controlled. They certainly vary a great deal according to the location and the quality of the accommodation. In 1970 more than £7 per square foot per year was being paid under new leases for the best West End offices and around £10 in the City, though most reasonably good accommodation there was letting in the range £5–£8. In Manchester, on the other hand, new rents for the best offices in the centre of town barely reached £1.50. In Sussex and Hampshire good offices were let at rents below £1.

These geographical variations reflect differences in scarcity and so do variations through time. Office rents in the City, taking 1956 as 100, had risen to about 200 in 1964 according to an article by Mr Jack Rose in 'The Estates Gazette' of 29.1.71. At the end of 1964 there were

19.2 million square feet of office space completed and vacant or under construction in Greater London. A ban on speculative office building was then introduced. This had a big effect, so that by March 1970 there were only 5.7 million square feet completed and vacant or under construction. Rents in 1970 were around the 700 mark. Thus rents rose by 100 index points during 8 years when there was no special control and by 500 points during 6 years when such a control was effectively limiting the supply.

High buildings provide more floor space per unit of ground space than low buildings. Hence they can be regarded as the substitution of 'building' for 'site' in order to make accommodation less site-intensive. This illustrates the point that the scarcity of sites generates the substitution of other inputs. Since the height of buildings in this country has been subject to control for many years, variations within British cities do not match those in American cities. But the contrast between the density of development in our large cities and that in smaller provincial towns reflects a long-standing difference in scarcity. Once upon a time high buildings were only constructed to the greater glory of God, but after the invention of the lift the supply and demand for urban space became a second factor!

10.2. *The determinants of residential site values*

What this example does not demonstrate is the significance of the relationship between office site values and office rents in the working of the property market. Unfortunately, figures of office site values are hard to come by. However, the matter can be examined by looking at another part of the property market – new private houses and sites for house-building. Here too, planning regulates what may be done but prices are not controlled. The same phenomenon of a greater site-intensity of building in response to a greater scarcity of sites can also be observed. By and large the Victorians only built flats in central areas. As building land subsequently grew scarcer the flats were built farther out. Where houses were put up, the gardens were smaller than those provided for the houses of earlier generations. The substitution of flats for houses and a reduction in the size of gardens both economize in the use of land.

For speculative builders neither sites nor building materials are durable inputs. They acquire both, build, and then sell the houses. Hence their demand for sites – which is what determines site values, given the supply – is a *derived* demand for an input. If the most suitable kind of house to build on a particular site will, in a builder's opinion, sell for £9,000 and if he puts the cost of building it at £6,000, then he will make a profit if he can obtain the site at less than £3,000. How much he actually offers for the site, supposing it to be up for sale, will depend partly on how much other builders may be expected to offer. If the site is auctioned he will be ready to go up to a price just sufficiently below £3,000 to give him the minimum profit which would just make the operation worth his while. Other builders will generally reckon in a very similar manner, so if there is nothing unusual about the site it will sell for a price which leaves the purchaser a normal-sized profit on a £9,000 house.

This simple example suggests that the price which can be obtained for a site with planning permission for housing depends upon:

- the number of houses allowed to be built upon it by the planning authority;
- the estimated selling prices of the most appropriate types of dwelling to be put up on it;
- the costs of building these dwellings and the normal rate of profit obtained by speculative builders.

There is freedom of entry and plenty of competition in speculative building, so the normal rate of profit probably does not vary very much from one builder to another. Profits will, of course, be higher for the more efficient builders, but in proportion to their lower costs. The main variation between sites under the third factor will therefore be on account of the type of dwelling. A house (or flat) which will sell for a larger price will cost more to build if the higher price reflects a larger size. But if one house will sell at a higher price than another only because its site is better located, it will not cost more to build. Hence the *difference* between selling price and building cost will be greater in high house-price areas than in low house-price areas. But it is this difference that determines the value of a house site. So the theory is that the value of a site for one house will be greater where houses are expensive than where they are (relatively) cheap.

The planning authorities regulate housing density so that the number of houses permitted on a particular piece of building land is normally lower than would be most profitable. It ought to follow from this that, where a higher density is allowed, the value of building land will (other things equal) be higher.

Our analysis enables us to make yet a third prediction. Economic growth, we said, raises the demand for urban accommodation relative to the supply. On the other hand it has not, over the last decade or so, raised the index of building costs any faster than the index of the prices of manufactured goods. Hence the prices of new houses have been rising faster than the costs of building them. Official statistics give the 1963–9 rise for Great Britain in the average price of new homes for private owners as 51% and the rise in the cost of new construction over the same period as 23%. It should follow that the prices paid for building land with planning permission have been rising very steeply and an official index of private sector housing land prices in England and Wales does indeed show a doubling in the price per plot over the same period.

10.3. *Site values round London*

An analysis of auction results for building land in the two pairs of years 1963–4 and 1968–9 published by Mr John McAuslan in 'The Estates Gazette' of 11.4.70 enables us to test all three predictions. The figures in the table relate to the London region. Though housing land here is much more valuable than elsewhere, the official index shows it to have been rising more slowly than in other parts of England and Wales. Similarly, though houses are more expensive in London than elsewhere, it appears that the rate of increase in their prices in the latter half of the sixties was lower than in most other parts of the country. Since, for almost any given type of house, prices are higher in an Inner Ring around London than in an Outer Ring, we expect land values to be higher in the Inner Ring too. This and the other two predictions are abundantly confirmed: the table shows (i) that prices were higher in the Inner Ring, (ii) that they have risen steeply, and (iii) that they have been higher where denser development is permitted.

PRICE PER ACRE OF LONDON BUILDING LAND, £

| | Dwellings per acre permitted | | | | |
	4–7	8–12	13–18	19–25	26+
Inner Ring (0–20 miles)					
1963–4	9,684	19,600	28,000	28,600	44,000
1968–9	16,638	24,200	45,100	44,000	55,000
Outer Ring (21–40 miles)					
1963–4	8,222	12,000	15,000	17,500	–
1968–9	16,500	21,710	–	31,500	–

One point remains to be made. It is that to any one builder alone it may appear that land values determine house prices. From his point of view there is a going price to be paid for land, just as there is for bricks and for bricklayers. Thus he can regard what he pays for all his inputs as determining the cost which he has to recover in the price of his product. It seems to follow that a rise in any of these items, including land values, will increase the prices of new houses. *But this is to put matters the wrong way round for analysis of the market as a whole.* What appears to be the case for the individual builder does *not* hold on the aggregate level. The values of sites depend upon the demands for them of *all* the competing builders, and these demands are derived from the demand for houses.

What we have been talking about is related to the theory of 'rent'. When first developed by Ricardo it related to the rent of agricultural land. Refinement by successive generations of economists has made the 'rent' of economic theory different from rent in the everyday sense. An economist, for example, may claim that much of the Beatles' earnings has been 'rent', although some rents are also 'rent'. In this chapter I have not tried to explain 'rent', since it is a rather platitudinous theory best reserved for orthodox textbooks. It is, in any case, often possible to explain how the economy works without using a private language.

CONCLUSION

There are no 'iron laws' of demand and supply. How demand and supply are adjusted to one another varies from case to case, as this book has endeavoured to show. If there is one central theme it is the importance of substitution.

Index

ECONOMIC CONCEPTS